THE STOIC WISDOM
of
EPICTETUS

Practical Lessons
from the Enchiridion
for Modern Life

RICHARD LAWSON

ISBN 978-1-961963-99-3
Published by Karma Studio
info@karmabookshelf.com

Contents

"It is not things themselves that disturb us, but our judgments about things."

—— Epictetus, Enchiridion, §5

Introduction

Most people approach Stoicism looking for relief. Epictetus begins by denying it.

He doesn't offer reflection, reassurance, or consolation. He speaks in rules. This isn't a stylistic preference. It's a deliberate refusal to soften distinctions that determine whether judgment holds or collapses under pressure.

Many readers come to Stoicism expecting perspective or calm. Epictetus offers neither as a starting point. He begins with limits. What belongs to you. What never does. What can be trained. What can't be secured. His teaching doesn't aim to make life feel better. It aims to make judgment accurate.

This book's written with that aim.

For Epictetus, philosophy is discipline, not outlook. He assumes most distress is self-produced through confusion about responsibility and control. His response isn't encouragement but correction. When a belief fails under strain, he removes it. When a habit of thought creates dependency, he cuts it back to its source. The result can feel severe. It's meant to.

That severity serves a specific purpose: freedom. Not freedom from difficulty, but freedom from being governed by what can't be commanded. Epictetus doesn't promise relief from events. He insists on independence from them. The cost of that independence is precision. The benefit is stability that doesn't depend on circumstances improving.

This approach sets Epictetus apart within the Stoic tradition. Marcus Aurelius writes to steady himself while bearing responsibility. Seneca writes to counsel others through complexity and emotion. Epictetus teaches students how to train judgment so that neither position nor loss determines their inner order. He's less expansive, more demanding, and intentionally repetitive because training requires it.

Accordingly, this book doesn't present Stoicism as a philosophy to admire or a mindset to adopt. It treats Epictetus as a teacher of mental discipline. His ideas are organized here as rules that can be tested in daily life—at work, in conflict, under uncertainty—without appeal to comfort or inspiration. The explanations are firm by design. They aim to remove confusion, not to motivate.

The chapters that follow assume an intelligent reader willing to accept constraint. They don't argue for Stoicism. They show how its discipline functions when applied consistently. If the rules feel narrow, that's because they are. Epictetus reduces philosophy to what can actually be held when pressure rises.

What follows begins with the foundation of his teaching. Everything else depends on it.

A Note on Sources and Language

The quotations attributed to Epictetus in this book are presented in modern English. They're not intended as literal translations. They're interpretive renderings based primarily on the Enchiridion and the Discourses, aimed at clarity and practical use rather than textual fidelity.

No single English edition's been followed line by line. The wording's been shaped to preserve function: to reflect how the rules are meant to act on judgment, not how they appear on the page.

Primary source texts are in the public domain. A reference edition's provided at the end of the book for readers who wish to consult the original material directly.

PART I

THE DOMAIN
OF CONTROL

Chapter 1

Why Epictetus Begins Here

Epictetus is often introduced with a single fact: he was born a slave.

The detail is true, but it's not enough—and taken alone, it can distort how his work is read.

The difficulty of Epictetus doesn't come from his background. It comes from his method. His teaching isn't an extension of personal hardship, nor does it trade on endurance as moral authority. The conditions of his life account for his precision, not for the force of his claims. What gives weight to his words is the narrowness of what he's willing to call freedom.

He lived in the first century of the Roman Empire, within a structure defined by hierarchy, dependence, and public status. Legal standing governed access, protection, and voice. Control over circumstances was limited even for those at the top. For most, it was absent altogether. Epictetus encountered this order directly—first as property within another man's household, later as a teacher whose position still relied on tolerance and patronage. Autonomy was never assumed.

Freedom, in this setting, couldn't be treated as a political condition or a private feeling. It had to be located precisely or not claimed at all. Epictetus approaches it as a boundary. Either something depends on you, or it doesn't. When peace is attached to what cannot be secured, disturbance follows as a consequence rather than an accident.

After gaining his freedom, Epictetus studied philosophy in Rome and later taught in Nicopolis. His instruction took place in person, among students who presented themselves for correction rather than discussion. Nothing in that setting required persuasion. What was required was clarity. The tone of his teaching reflects this. These weren't essays composed for a public audience, but lessons delivered to those already willing to be challenged.

The starting point of his philosophy reflects that demand. He doesn't prepare the ground with encouragement or gradual concessions. He establishes the limit that governs everything else. Before emotion, before action, before endurance, one requirement is fixed: responsibility must be placed exactly where command is possible. Without that placement, no further instruction holds.

This compression is intentional. Epictetus reduces philosophy to what remains usable under pressure. Beliefs that rely on favorable conditions are discarded. Any account of freedom that depends on outcomes is set aside. What survives is narrow by design. It has to be.

The opening distinction is left uncompromised because compromise would render it unusable. A rule that holds only when conditions are favorable isn't a rule. It's a preference waiting to be overturned.

Epictetus begins by separating what depends on you from what doesn't. The separation isn't proposed as a helpful frame or a way of thinking about events. It's treated as a boundary that governs responsibility. Whatever is placed beyond that boundary remains exposed to chance. Attaching peace to it introduces instability, not because the object is harmful, but because it cannot be secured.

For this reason, entry into the discipline isn't gradual. The distinction operates in full or not at all. As long as outcomes, reputation, or the responses of others are treated as controllable, frustration is misread as injustice. Pressure is experienced as interference rather than as correction. The work begins only when responsibility is confined to what can actually be commanded.

The refusal to soften this point is often mistaken for severity. In fact, it reflects how quickly confusion forms when responsibility is dispersed. Claiming ownership over externals doesn't increase influence. It increases exposure. Stability becomes conditional. Attention fragments between what can be shaped and what cannot.

The method counters this exposure by contracting the field of concern. Control is not expanded inward to compensate for external limits. Responsibility is narrowed until it fits exactly. Judgment, choice, and intention remain available under every circumstance. Everything else fluctuates.

This narrowing alters the character of action. It doesn't remove involvement, and it doesn't diminish care. It redirects concern toward what can be governed without distortion. When attention is aligned with that limit, action steadies. When it drifts beyond it, agitation follows predictably.

The rule must precede everything that comes after. Without it, later instructions lose force and collapse into advice. With it, each situation functions as a test. The placement of judgment is either confirmed or exposed, again and again.

The resistance provoked by this opening rule doesn't arise from its difficulty, but from its implications. Once the boundary is accepted, much of what had been treated as stable is revealed as contingent. Outcomes lose authority. Approval ceases to function as protection. Effort is separated from result. What remains exposed to chance is seen as such.

This shift is often experienced as loss. In fact, it's a correction. What falls away was never secure enough to support judgment. Epictetus doesn't attempt to cushion this realization. He treats clarity as something that must withstand friction. If the distinction holds only when circumstances cooperate, it hasn't been grasped.

Attention is directed inward, but not as retreat. Judgment becomes the primary site of responsibility because it's the only site that remains accessible without interruption. This doesn't narrow life. It restores proportion. What lies outside command is treated according to its nature. What depends on choice is held to account.

The order of instruction follows from this correction. Confusion is removed before difficulty is addressed. Without that removal, endurance hardens into stubbornness and restraint collapses into suppression. The rule doesn't prepare the way for comfort. It prepares the way for use.

The opening distinction doesn't reassure. It orients. Once responsibility is placed where it belongs, the rest of Epictetus' teaching proceeds without qualification. Without that placement, none of it can function.

This is where Epictetus begins.

Chapter 2

What You Are Mistaking for Control

Once the boundary is drawn, attention turns outward—not to expand responsibility, but to see where it's been misplaced. Most confusion doesn't come from denying the rule, but from applying it inconsistently. Certain things continue to be treated as controllable, not because they are, but because they're familiar, visible, or emotionally charged.

This chapter addresses those confusions directly. Not to catalog externals exhaustively, but to show how easily responsibility drifts beyond its proper domain, and what that drift costs when left uncorrected.

What You Treat as Yours

Certain things continue to be treated as controllable even after the boundary has been stated. Not because they belong there, but because they're familiar, visible, and reinforced by habit. Results, reputation, approval, health, and circumstance retain a false sense of ownership long after responsibility has been narrowed.

The confusion doesn't announce itself. Effort extends quietly into outcome. Intention begins to depend on response. Standing gets handled as something you can secure through vigilance or performance. None of this feels excessive. It feels practical. That's why it persists.

These things aren't identified as externals to encourage distance from life. They're identified to correct attribution. When you treat an outcome as owned, judgment invests itself in what cannot be commanded. Success begins to feel personal. Failure registers as loss rather than occurrence. The weight isn't incidental—it's structural.

Reputation operates the same way. It appears close enough to manage while remaining dependent on factors that never settle. Attention drifts toward impression and anticipation. Judgment adjusts itself to preserve standing. The result? Continuous vigilance, reactive and exposed.

Even conditions that feel most intimate follow the same pattern. Health, energy, and circumstance are often handled as extensions of effort or character. When they shift, judgment searches for explanation or fault. The response mirrors ownership, not contingency.

Nothing here is framed as moral failure. The error lies in placement. Responsibility has been assigned where authority doesn't fully reach. That assignment produces tension, defensiveness, and sustained monitoring of what cannot be held.

The Cost of Misplaced Responsibility

When responsibility extends beyond what can be commanded, its effects register immediately in judgment. Minor disruptions take on disproportionate weight. Delays feel personal. Outcomes begin to define competence rather than test it. The mind reacts as if something owed has been withheld.

A pattern forms. Attention shifts outward, tracking conditions, responses, and signs of approval. Effort entangles itself with expectation. Action is no longer assessed by whether it was chosen well, but by whether it was rewarded. Stability gives way to calculation. Calm becomes conditional.

Over time, this conditionality hardens. Success encourages attachment instead of confidence. Failure invites justification instead of correction. Judgment learns to anticipate disturbance and adjusts itself in advance. Caution masks dependency. Ambition signals exposure to chance.

The cost reaches beyond emotion. Decision-making degrades. Choices stall while outcomes are imagined. Standards bend to accommodate response. Integrity becomes negotiable when its consequences seem uncertain. None of this requires dramatic circumstances. It unfolds under ordinary pressure applied to misplaced ownership.

This pattern is treated as a technical error, not a character flaw. Responsibility has been assigned where authority doesn't reach. The resulting instability follows from structure, not temperament. Correction doesn't demand greater effort—it requires contraction.

When responsibility is returned to its proper domain, much of this strain releases on its own. Attention steadies. Action simplifies. Outcomes resume their proper place as occurrences rather than verdicts. What remains exposed to chance stops being asked to provide security.

PART II

JUDGMENT
AND PERCEPTION

Chapter 3

How Judgments Distort Reality

Disturbance doesn't originate in what happens. The source is the judgment about what happens. Between event and reaction, something intervenes—the meaning assigned to what occurs, the weight given to it, the authority granted to that assessment.

A judgment classifies what appears, assigns consequence, and allows a conclusion to stand. Once assent is given, reaction follows with the force of necessity. What feels automatic is usually the result of agreement that went unexamined.

This clarity comes only after responsibility has been confined to its proper domain. Treat judgment as active rather than passive, and impressions lose their authority to compel. Appearance and acceptance separate. Reaction becomes traceable to a decision, not to the event itself.

Distortion doesn't arise from events, but from the way they're received and affirmed. Judgment enters before reaction and determines its course.

"It is not events that disturb people, but their judgments about them."

Enchiridion 5

What Epictetus Meant

Disturbance doesn't originate in what happens. It forms in how what happens gets interpreted. An event presents itself without meaning attached. Judgment supplies that meaning and then treats it as fact. Once this occurs, reaction follows as if compelled.

The correction isn't about minimizing difficulty. It's about identifying where disturbance is produced. Judgment assigns harm, insult, or threat where none is inherent, and the resulting agitation is self-generated. The correction lies not in changing events, but in examining the judgment that's been allowed to stand.

Two people experience the same delay. One judges it as obstruction—time stolen, respect denied. The other judges it as circumstance—neutral, temporary, requiring adjustment but not interpretation. The delay itself carries no inherent meaning. The difference in their responses traces directly to the judgment each formed about what the delay meant.

Why This Still Matters

Reactions feel unavoidable because the judgment producing them passes unnoticed. Anger, anxiety, and resentment appear to be responses to circumstances, when they're responses to conclusions reached too quickly. As long as judgment remains invisible, it can't be corrected. The cost is repeated disturbance attributed to the world rather than to interpretation.

How to Apply This Today

Place attention on the conclusion forming behind the reaction. Instead of asking what happened, notice what's being asserted about what happened. Disturbance begins where that assertion is treated as unquestionable.

Track one recurring reaction this week. Write down the event, then separately write what you concluded about the event. The gap between the two is where judgment operates. Most people discover the conclusion contains far more than the event itself supplied.

"When something appears painful or frightening, remember that it is not the thing itself, but your judgment about it."

Enchiridion 5

What Epictetus Meant

Impressions arrive with force. They announce themselves as urgent, threatening, or harmful. The appearance alone doesn't disturb. Disturbance begins when the impression is accepted as a verdict rather than as information.

Separating what appears from what is concluded exposes the exact moment where assent turns sensation into distress. The work isn't to suppress impressions, but to withhold agreement until judgment has been examined.

Why This Still Matters

Fear and aversion often feel justified because the impression presenting them feels immediate. The speed of that presentation disguises the act of assent. Impressions treated as facts rather than proposals mean reaction hardens before clarity has a chance to intervene. This leads to patterns of avoidance and defensiveness that feel protective but produce instability.

The speed is the trap. An impression of danger arrives, and the mind has already agreed with it before examination was possible. What felt like a response to threat was actually a response to an unexamined conclusion about threat. The slower the agreement, the more often the examination reveals the gap between appearance and fact.

How to Apply This Today

When impressions arrive with urgency, allow a brief pause between appearance and agreement. This prevents judgment from being finalized by momentum. What appears compelling doesn't need to be treated as decisive.

Choose one category of impression you respond to quickly—criticism, dismissal, unexpected change. For one week, practice inserting a three-second pause before responding. Not to change the response, just to notice whether you're agreeing with the impression before examining what it's actually claiming.

"First, do not give way to the impression; then, examine the impression and do not let it carry you away before you have done so."

Discourses 2.18.8

What Epictetus Meant

The sequence matters as much as the instruction. Two steps, in order: first, don't yield; second, examine. Yielding before examination means reaction has already been determined by the time inspection begins. The examination becomes rationalization rather than judgment.

This isn't resistance to impressions. It's refusal to finalize assent before review is complete. Impressions present themselves with claims about value, threat, or significance and press for immediate acceptance. Interrupting that pressure—just long enough for examination to occur—is where judgment recovers its function.

Why This Still Matters

Much behavior is shaped by impressions that are never questioned. Once accepted, they dictate reaction and reinforce themselves through repetition. Over time, this creates a sense of inevitability around certain emotions or responses. Agency doesn't disappear—it just gets surrendered at the moment the impression is accepted without examination.

The pattern becomes self-reinforcing. An impression presents disrespect. You accept the claim without examination. Defensiveness follows. The next similar impression finds easier acceptance because the response pattern is already established. What started as a single unexamined judgment becomes a default mode of reaction.

How to Apply This Today

During a moment of perceived insult, an impression arises asserting disrespect or threat. Before reacting, identify what's being claimed. That pause alone often reveals how much has been added beyond what actually occurred.

Ask: "What exactly is this impression claiming?" Not what happened—what the impression asserts it means. An email goes unanswered. The event: no reply. The impression's claim: you're being ignored, dismissed, deprioritized. Examining that claim often shows it's been accepted without evidence. The event is real. The interpretation is optional.

"...you have the power to wipe out this judgment now."

Enchiridion 20

What Epictetus Meant

The judgment that produced the disturbance wasn't delivered from outside. It was made. Which means it can be unmade. The distress felt in the present isn't a fixed property of the situation—it's a property of the assessment currently applied to it. Withdraw the assessment, and the distress doesn't have a foundation to rest on.

This isn't denial. The situation remains. What changes is the judgment standing over it. The power to wipe out the judgment now isn't a technique for avoiding difficulty. It's recognition that the judgment was never required in the first place—it was added, and it can be removed.

Why This Still Matters

Disturbance persists when impressions are treated as descriptions of fixed reality rather than as assessments that remain open to revision. Distress that feels like a property of events is actually a property of interpretation. This matters practically: it means the source of the disturbance is where intervention remains possible.

Once the judgment is seen as the source rather than the event, the target of correction shifts inward—where adjustment can actually occur.

How to Apply This Today

Shift attention from how something appears to what judgment is currently applied to it. What arrives can be acknowledged without granting authority to the conclusion attached to it.

When disturbance is present, ask: "What judgment am I holding about this situation?" Name it explicitly. Then ask: "Is this judgment required, or did I add it?" That distinction often reveals the judgment as something chosen rather than inevitable. Chosen judgments can be revised. The disturbance doesn't have to wait for the situation to change.

"What is it that troubles us? Our opinions. What is it that makes us restless and fearful? Our opinions."

Discourses 3.3.14

What Epictetus Meant

The repetition is deliberate. Asking twice removes the possibility of dismissing the first answer. If only asked once, the mind might absorb it as a general observation and move on. Asked twice, it becomes a direct accusation: the trouble is yours. The restlessness is yours. The fear is yours. Not because events produced them, but because opinion supplied them.

Opinion here means the judgment held about what a situation means, what it requires, what it threatens. Restlessness and fear don't arise from facts—they arise from the story built around facts. That story is opinion. Opinion is revisable.

Why This Still Matters

When agitation is attributed to circumstances, the response is to change circumstances. This is often impossible, always costly, and frequently unsuccessful. Agitation often originates in what judgment adds rather than in what is present. The same event produces different reactions depending on what judgment supplies.

When additions go unnoticed, agitation feels justified. When they're seen for what they are—opinions, not facts—their necessity weakens. The event hasn't changed. The opinion about it has. That shift is available immediately, without requiring anything outside to cooperate.

How to Apply This Today

During a sudden setback, an impression arises asserting failure or consequence. Notice what's being added—finality, threat, judgment of self. Identify the opinion explicitly: not "this is bad," but "I have formed the opinion that this is bad." The shift from description to opinion introduces a small but decisive gap. The reaction often loosens.

Write down one source of current restlessness. Now complete this sentence: "I am restless because I hold the opinion that..." The opinion becomes visible. Visible opinions can be questioned. Unnoticed ones cannot.

"Every error involves a contradiction; for since he who errs does not wish to err but to act rightly, it is plain that he is not doing what he wishes."

Discourses 1.18.1

What Epictetus Meant

No one chooses to react badly. People react badly because judgment has formed a mistaken assessment and assent followed from it. The error isn't in the desire—everyone desires to act well. The error is in what judgment has concluded about the situation, about what it requires, about what is actually happening.

This reframes harshness toward others and toward oneself. Someone who reacts with anger, defensiveness, or poor judgment isn't doing so from a position of clarity. They're acting from a mistaken impression they've already agreed with. The problem isn't character—it's the unexamined judgment driving the response.

Why This Still Matters

When reactions feel immediate, they're experienced as inevitable. Emotion feels imposed rather than chosen. This obscures responsibility and reinforces the belief that certain responses are unavoidable. But unavoidable reactions are simply reactions where the judgment preceding them moved too fast to catch.

Each automatic assent makes the next one more likely. What began as a single moment of unexamined agreement becomes a habit of response that operates below awareness. The person reacting defensively to criticism isn't only responding to the current criticism—they're responding through a pattern of assent built over dozens of similar moments, none examined at the time.

How to Apply This Today

Treat assent as a separate act from the moment reaction surfaces. This restores a point of intervention that would otherwise be missed.

Start with one category. If you react strongly to perceived criticism, make that your focus for one week. Each time an impression of criticism arises, pause before assenting. Don't try to change the reaction—just identify the moment of assent. Awareness alone begins to interrupt the automaticity. Over time, the gap between impression and response widens enough for judgment to function.

"Do not be deceived by the appearance of things."

Enchiridion 16

What Epictetus Meant

Appearances carry implied conclusions. Something looks threatening, final, or significant, and judgment accepts that framing without inspection. Deception here isn't external manipulation—it's self-generated, produced by assent granted too quickly to what shows up.

Impressions arrive incomplete. Judgment completes them by adding meaning, threat, or evaluation. Once that addition is made, the impression gains force. Without it, the impression remains inert. The instruction names the mechanism: deception enters through appearances accepted before they're examined. Guard the gate, and the deception doesn't get through.

Why This Still Matters

Urgent impressions often bypass review. Force isn't evidence. An impression can arrive with urgency, clarity, or emotional weight and still be misleading. Treating intensity as reliability removes judgment from its proper role. This produces cycles of overreaction that feel justified by how strongly something appeared.

The misdirection compounds over time. Energy goes toward managing circumstances, curating environments, avoiding triggers—all attempts to prevent impressions from arising. Meanwhile, the actual mechanism of disturbance—assent—continues operating unexamined. External conditions become increasingly necessary while capacity to handle unfavorable impressions through proper judgment deteriorates.

How to Apply This Today

Allow impressions to arrive without treating them as instructions. Urgency isn't a reason to accept. Strength of appearance isn't a reason to agree.

Track this for three days. Each time you notice a strong reaction, write down: (1) the impression that arose, (2) what it claimed, (3) whether you granted assent before examining the claim. Certain categories of impression tend to receive automatic assent while others get examined naturally. Identifying the automatic categories is where intervention becomes possible.

Before any action guided by a strong impression, run three questions: What is this impression claiming? Is that claim verified by anything beyond how strongly it presented itself? What would I choose if I weren't operating under the force of this claim? The entire process takes seconds—but it introduces a gap where none existed before.

Chapter 4

Withholding Assent

Assent is the point where judgment either retains authority or relinquishes it. Impressions don't determine action on their own. They acquire force only when agreement is granted. What follows is decided at that moment.

Assent is often mistaken for something passive, as if conclusions form automatically once something appears convincing. Agreement is an act. It's given, not received. Even when it happens quickly, it happens as judgment's response to a claim.

This distinction changes how responsibility is understood. If assent is active, then disturbance isn't imposed—it's produced. Reaction no longer belongs to events or impressions, but to the decision that allowed their claims to stand.

Withholding assent doesn't require suppression or delay for its own sake. It requires restraint at the precise point where judgment is asked to confirm what appears. That restraint isn't hesitation. It's discipline.

"Guard yourself against being carried away by the impression; let the matter wait a little, and give yourself a space."

Enchiridion 34

What Epictetus Meant

The instruction is physical before it's philosophical: create space. Impressions carry momentum. They arrive with implied urgency and press for immediate confirmation. The space referred to isn't delay for its own sake—it's the interval in which judgment can operate rather than simply follow.

Being "carried away" is precise. The image is of a current pulling someone downstream before they've decided to swim. Agreement granted under the force of an impression is still agreement—but it's agreement without examination, which means it's agreement without judgment. The space between impression and assent is where judgment exists at all.

Think of a message that provokes immediate anger. The impression arrives: disrespect, dismissal, threat. Everything about the impression presses for instant response. The person who waits—even briefly—has preserved something the person who responds immediately has surrendered. Not the right to respond. The authority over how.

Why This Still Matters

Reactive patterns feel natural because the interval between impression and response has closed through habit. Once it closes, response and impression become indistinguishable. What's happening looks like feeling, but it's judgment operating on a very short cycle—fast enough to be invisible, not fast enough to be reliable.

Giving yourself a space isn't weakness. Speed that bypasses examination isn't decisiveness. It's impression management—impressions managing judgment, rather than the other way around.

How to Apply This Today

Identify one situation this week where you responded faster than you examined. Not the worst reaction—any one. Trace it back: where did the impression arrive, and how quickly did agreement follow? The gap between those two moments is where practice lives.

Next time a strong impression arrives, use a physical marker before responding—stand up, get water, change rooms. Not to avoid the impression. To restore the space that carries judgment with it.

"Practice saying to every unpleasing impression: 'You are an impression and not at all the thing you appear to be.'"

Discourses 3.12.7

What Epictetus Meant

The command is to practice, not to believe. Recognizing an impression as an impression rather than as the thing it presents itself to be is a trained capacity, not a natural one. Left untrained, impressions arrive already wearing the authority of facts. The practice strips that authority before it gets confirmed.

"Unpleasing" is the category where this matters most. Pleasant impressions rarely cause problems—they're accepted readily and their consequences are usually manageable. Unpleasing impressions arrive with urgency and threat and press hardest for immediate assent. That's precisely why they require the most deliberate interruption.

The phrase itself does the work. Saying "you are an impression" to what seems like an established fact introduces a wedge between appearance and conclusion. Not disbelief—just refusal to treat the appearance as the final word before examination.

Why This Still Matters

Without this practice, impressions claim the status of reality by default. Anger feels like an appropriate response to an actual insult—not a response to the impression that an insult occurred. Fear feels like a rational reaction to actual danger—not a reaction to the impression of danger. The feeling is real. The claim the impression makes about its source is what requires verification.

The habit builds unevenly. Some categories of impression get examined naturally; others bypass review entirely. Identifying which categories receive automatic assent—and then practicing the interruption specifically there—is where the work is actually located.

How to Apply This Today

Choose one recurring unpleasant impression—a type of situation that reliably produces a strong reaction. For one week, practice the phrase each time it arises. Not as a calming technique. As a factual correction to an implicit claim.

Track what changes. The impression itself won't stop arriving. What may shift is the authority it carries—from automatic verdict to proposal requiring examination. That shift is what the practice is building.

"Every habit and faculty is preserved and increased by the corresponding actions: the habit of walking, by walking; of running, by running."

Discourses 2.18.1

What Epictetus Meant

Withholding assent isn't a decision made once—it's a capacity built through repetition. What applies to physical habits applies to habits of judgment: the faculty is preserved or eroded depending on how it's exercised. Every time assent is withheld appropriately, the faculty strengthens. Every time it yields without examination, it weakens.

The reverse also holds, and this is the warning embedded in the principle. The habit of giving assent too quickly is also built through repetition. Each automatic agreement makes the next one more likely. Each yielded interval makes the next interval harder to find. This is why reactive patterns feel fixed—they've been trained, not inherited.

Why This Still Matters

People often treat restraint as something that should be available on demand, without training. Under low pressure, perhaps. Under high pressure—when impressions are strongest and most urgent—the capacity to withhold assent depends entirely on whether it's been practiced under lower pressure first.

The faculty doesn't appear when needed. It appears if it's been maintained. This makes the question practical: what's being practiced right now, in ordinary situations, that will either support or undermine judgment when the stakes rise?

How to Apply This Today

Don't start with high-stakes situations. Start with small ones where the impulse to agree automatically is present but mild—a minor irritation, a routine frustration, a small impatience. Withhold assent there. Not because those situations matter enormously, but because the faculty gets built there.

Keep a brief record for two weeks: situations where you withheld assent and situations where you gave it without examination. The pattern reveals what habit is actually being trained. Adjust from there.

"In every affair consider what precedes and follows, and then undertake it."

Enchiridion 29

What Epictetus Meant

The instruction targets the most common failure point: beginning without understanding what's been entered into. Assent granted to an impression commits judgment to everything that follows from that impression. Most people grant the assent and then discover the implications—after the commitment has been made and reversal is costly.

Considering what precedes means examining the impression itself: what is it actually claiming, and is that claim verified? Considering what follows means examining where assent leads: what response will this agreement produce, and is that the response I would choose with examination rather than without it?

Both steps happen before undertaking—before the assent is given. This is the sequence: examine, then agree. Not agree, then examine what I've agreed to.

Why This Still Matters

Premature assent creates obligations that feel external but were self-imposed. Someone agrees to an impression of urgency, responds immediately, and then experiences the consequences of that response as if circumstances produced them. But the sequence started with agreement. The circumstances didn't press for the response—the impression claimed they did, and judgment agreed.

Tracing obligations back to the assent that created them is clarifying. Some were examined before agreement. Many weren't. The ones that feel most constraining are usually the ones where assent outran examination most quickly.

How to Apply This Today

Before responding to anything that produces a strong impression—a request, a provocation, an apparent problem—run the two questions: What is this impression claiming? Where does agreement lead? Both questions together take less than a minute. What they produce is a response from judgment rather than a reaction from momentum.

Pick one obligation that currently feels burdensome. When did you agree to it, and what exactly were you agreeing to? The distinction between what you agreed to and what you're now experiencing often clarifies whether the burden comes from the commitment or from how the impression of it has expanded since.

"What is good? Knowledge of how to choose. What is evil? Ignorance of how to choose."

Discourses 2.8.29

What Epictetus Meant

Knowledge of how to choose places the decisive capacity inside judgment, not inside circumstances. Choice isn't made by events—it's made by the quality of judgment exercised in response to them. Good and evil aren't properties of what happens but of how assent is managed in relation to what happens.

Ignorance of how to choose isn't stupidity—it's the absence of practiced examination. Someone who yields to every impression without scrutiny hasn't chosen badly. They haven't chosen at all. They've followed. The problem isn't that they wanted wrong things; it's that they allowed impressions to determine the wanting before judgment had the chance to intervene.

Why This Still Matters

This reframes what's at stake when assent is granted carelessly. The cost isn't just a bad reaction in the moment—it's erosion of the capacity to choose at all. Each automatic assent is practice in not choosing. Over time, the feeling of agency in one's own responses diminishes, not because choice was taken away, but because the habit of exercising it was allowed to weaken.

The flip side matters equally. Each withheld assent—each moment where judgment pauses before confirming what appears—is practice in actually choosing. The faculty is either maintained or abandoned through use.

How to Apply This Today

Examine one decision from the past week that felt reactive—where you responded without quite meaning to. Identify what you agreed to in that moment and what the alternative would have been. Not to regret the response. To see the exact point where choice was available and wasn't exercised.

That point exists in every strong reaction. Locating it isn't about blame. It's about building the map of where examination can actually intervene—so that next time, judgment is present at the moment that matters rather than arriving afterward.

"I ought not to give assent to what is false."

Discourses 2.23.42

What Epictetus Meant

The statement is minimal and therefore precise. Not "I should withhold assent when uncertain"—that would make examination about doubt. Not "I should examine carefully"—that would make it about process. This is about obligation. Giving assent to what is false is a failure of judgment, not a misfortune.

The implied corollary: if assent to the false is an obligation to refuse, then examination isn't optional. It's the only way to distinguish what is false from what merely appears true. Impressions don't arrive labeled. What shows up carries whatever authority the situation lends it. Examination is the mechanism by which that authority is either confirmed or withdrawn.

Why This Still Matters

Most harmful reactions aren't based on what actually happened—they're based on false conclusions accepted without examination. Someone who responds with anger to a perceived slight has given assent to the claim that a slight occurred. That claim may be false. The anger is real; its basis may not be.

Treating assent to false impressions as a failure—not a mistake, not a lapse, but a failure of the faculty whose job is to verify—restores the weight that examination deserves. It's not a nice-to-have. It's the obligation that makes judgment what it claims to be.

How to Apply This Today

After a reaction that felt disproportionate, ask one question: "What did I agree to that may not have been true?" Not to dismiss the feeling. To identify the false assent that may have produced it.

Disproportionate reactions nearly always trace to an impression that contained more than the situation supplied. The anger was real; the insult may have been assumed. The fear was real; the danger may have been added. Finding the false claim doesn't erase the reaction—but it changes where responsibility is located, and where correction can begin.

"We ought not to give credence to every opinion of every person."

Discourses 1.7.32

What Epictetus Meant

Discrimination precedes credence. Not every impression deserves assent, not because it can be dismissed without examination, but because examination is precisely what establishes whether credence is warranted. Giving credence to every opinion means treating all impressions as equally authoritative—which effectively means treating none of them as subject to judgment at all.

The principle applies inward as much as outward. The "opinion of every person" includes one's own immediate impressions. Treating your own first reaction as a reliable account of what occurred is the same error as accepting whatever anyone tells you without examination. The impression isn't wrong because it's fast. It's unverified. Unverified isn't the same as false—but it isn't the same as true, either.

Why This Still Matters

The habit of indiscriminate credence is almost invisible to those who have it. Every reaction feels justified because the impression producing it was accepted without review, and accepted impressions feel like facts. From inside that pattern, there's no obvious difference between a reaction that followed examination and one that didn't—both feel equally warranted.

This is what makes discrimination both necessary and difficult. The cases where it matters most are exactly the cases where the impression feels most obviously correct. The most dangerous assents are the ones that feel like they didn't require examination at all.

How to Apply This Today

For one day, treat every strong impression as a proposal rather than a verdict—regardless of how obvious it seems. Not to doubt everything indiscriminately. To see how often "obvious" is doing the work that examination should be doing.

The day's experiment isn't about changing reactions. It's about noticing which reactions arrived pre-justified. Those are the ones where credence was granted without examination—and where the habit being built is either scrutiny or reflexive acceptance. Over time, the difference between those two habits is the difference between judgment and its absence.

PART III

DESIRE,
AVERSION,
AND FREEDOM

Chapter 5

Why Desire Creates Enslavement

With judgment clarified and assent restrained, desire becomes visible as a force rather than a feeling. It's not something to be managed, but something that directs attachment. What is desired is treated as necessary. What's treated as necessary begins to govern action.

Desire enslaves by fixing itself on what can't be secured. The issue isn't wanting, but wanting what lies outside command. Once desire reaches beyond judgment, it binds the mind to conditions it doesn't control. Satisfaction becomes conditional. Frustration becomes predictable.

Desire operates structurally. It draws judgment toward outcomes, approval, possession, or circumstance and presses for agreement before clarity has been established. Once desire is confirmed, assent follows with little resistance. What is wanted begins to set terms for what is tolerated, feared, or pursued.

Desire aligned with what depends on judgment steadies action. Desire directed outward creates dependence. The difference isn't emotional intensity, but placement.

"If you wish your children, and your wife, and your friends to live forever, you are stupid; for you wish the things which do not depend on you to depend on you, and the things which belong to others to be yours."

Enchiridion 14

What Epictetus Meant

The accusation isn't harsh—it's diagnostic. Wishing for what doesn't depend on you to depend on you isn't love or ambition. It's a structural error that guarantees suffering. The word "stupid" carries the Stoic meaning: acting against your own interest while believing you're acting for it.

Desire directed at externals—even beloved ones, even seemingly reasonable ones—creates a category error. You're treating what belongs to circumstance as if it belonged to you. The "ownership" that desire implies doesn't match the reality of what can actually be commanded. Desire claims authority over what it can't hold.

Think of the parent who desires their child to succeed in a specific way. The desire feels like love, and love it may be. But when the child's choices don't match the desired outcome, disturbance follows—not from the child's failure, but from a desire that claimed more than it could command. The love could remain; the specific demand is what produced the suffering.

Why This Still Matters

The error scales invisibly. Wanting a colleague to perform well, wanting a project to succeed, wanting a relationship to last—all reasonable desires. The problem appears when "want" becomes "require," when desire quietly assumes authority over what it can only hope for. That shift is where dependence forms, and most people don't notice it until the loss arrives.

How to Apply This Today

List three things you currently want that depend on others' choices or circumstances. For each one, notice how strongly "want" feels like "requires." That feeling is the bind. The desire hasn't changed the fact that these outcomes don't belong to you—but it's convinced judgment to act as if they do. What would remain of your engagement with each situation if you removed the requirement while keeping the preference?

"Remember that you must behave in life as at a dinner party. Is anything brought around to you? Put out your hand and take your share with moderation. Does it pass by you? Don't stop it. Is it not yet come? Don't stretch your desire towards it, but wait till it reaches you."

Enchiridion 15

What Epictetus Meant

The metaphor is precise, not decorative. At a dinner party, the dishes circulate according to the host's arrangement, not the guest's preference. Reaching across the table, demanding service, or hoarding what arrives—all violate the terms of the situation. The guest who understands this enjoys what comes. The one who doesn't exhausts themselves managing a situation they don't control.

Attention removed from what's available by reaching toward what hasn't arrived, or pulling back toward what's already passed—that removal is the cost. The reaching is the problem—not the wanting, but the extension of desire into territory where its authority doesn't exist. Moderation here isn't about eating less. It's about matching desire's reach to desire's actual jurisdiction.

Why This Still Matters

Restlessness has a structure. It appears when desire has already reached past what's present into what might come, or back into what was missed. Both movements remove attention from what actually depends on judgment now. Satisfaction keeps receding because desire keeps positioning itself ahead of what's available.

The cycle sustains itself. Each reached-for thing that arrives creates momentary satisfaction followed by new reaching. Each passed dish creates regret that focuses attention backward. Neither posture leaves room for genuine engagement with what's actually in front of you.

How to Apply This Today

For one week, track where your desire sits relative to what's actually in front of you. Is it reaching forward toward what hasn't arrived? Pulling back toward what's passed? Or settled in what's currently available? The exercise isn't to suppress wanting—it's to locate where desire is actually aimed at any given moment.

When you notice reaching, ask: "What's available right now that I'm not attending to because I'm looking elsewhere?" That question often reveals that what's present is being ignored in favor of what desire has decided should be here instead.

"Never say about anything, I have lost it; but, I have returned it. Is your child dead? It has been returned. Is your estate taken away? Well, and is not that likewise returned?"

Enchiridion 11

What Epictetus Meant

The reframe isn't consolation—it's correction. "Lost" implies prior ownership that was taken against your will. "Returned" implies temporary custody of what was never yours to keep permanently. The first framing guarantees grief when things end. The second framing doesn't—because it's accurate to the actual terms of possession.

Desire assumes ownership. When it fixes itself on a person, position, or possession, it treats that thing as belonging to the self. Loss then feels like theft. But the logic of possession was always flawed: external things are held temporarily, conditionally, subject to recall at any moment. Desire that acknowledges these terms in advance isn't less committed—it's more honest, and therefore less exposed when the terms reveal themselves.

Why This Still Matters

Grief over loss is real and appropriate. The disturbance being addressed here isn't grief itself—it's the additional suffering produced by desire that claimed permanent ownership of what it never had on those terms. "I was robbed" adds a layer of outrage to loss that "I held this for a time and now it's gone" doesn't.

The difference compounds over time. Every attachment that treats its object as permanent in principle creates a version of that claim. When loss eventually arrives—as it does—the debt comes due. The disturbance isn't just proportional to the loss; it's proportional to the gap between what desire claimed and what was actually available.

How to Apply This Today

Think of something you're currently attached to—a relationship, a role, a possession—and apply the reframe deliberately. Not "mine," but "held for now." Not "permanent," but "lent." Notice what shifts. The attachment doesn't have to disappear, but the claim changes—and with it, the exposure.

When loss occurs, try replacing "I have lost" with "I have returned" before reacting. Not to suppress feeling, but to notice how much of the disturbance comes from the expectation of permanent ownership rather than from the loss itself.

"How do we act in a voyage? We choose the pilot, the sailors, the hour. Then a storm arises. What concern is it of mine? I have discharged my duty; the rest is the business of the pilot."

Discourses 2.17.29

What Epictetus Meant

The voyage separates what belongs to action from what belongs to circumstance. Choosing pilot, sailors, and hour—all of these fall within command. The storm doesn't. The error desire makes is continuing past that boundary: treating the storm's behavior as part of the domain where action can determine outcomes.

"I have discharged my duty" is the decisive phrase. It closes the account at the boundary. Everything within the sailor's authority has been executed. What follows belongs to the pilot's judgment, the weather's indifference, the sea's terms. Desire that reaches past "I have discharged my duty" into "and therefore the voyage must succeed" has crossed from action into demand—and the crossing is where dependence forms.

This applies beyond voyages. You prepare the proposal carefully (yours). You deliver it well (yours). Whether it's accepted depends on the client's priorities, the timing, the budget cycle, the mood in the room (not yours). Desire that stops at "I prepared and delivered well" remains intact. Desire that requires the acceptance has extended into territory that was never available to it.

Why This Still Matters

Distinguishing your part from the rest isn't resignation—it's accuracy. Most frustration doesn't come from failing to do your part. It comes from doing your part and then demanding that the rest of the situation follow. The demand feels reasonable because effort was real. But the effort being real doesn't make the outcome commandable. Those are separate facts, and desire routinely conflates them.

Once effort and outcome are separated clearly, effort can be given fully without the disturbance that follows when outcomes don't cooperate. The work gets done well. The results remain what they are.

How to Apply This Today

Take one current goal and divide it explicitly: "What part is mine?" and "What part isn't?" Write both lists. The first list is where full effort belongs. The second list is what you're hoping for, but can't command.

Desire placed entirely on the first list is desire that can be satisfied through action. Desire that bleeds into the second list is desire that requires circumstances to cooperate. Notice how much of your current frustration with this goal lives in the second list—outcomes you're requiring rather than results you can produce. That's not where your authority is. The pilot handles the pilot's part. Discharge your own, and stop managing what belongs to the storm.

"Condition yourself, therefore, not to think of what you desire as necessary—for there are many things without which we can live and upon which chance has no power."

Discourses 4.4.33

What Epictetus Meant

"Necessary" is the word that converts desire into enslavement. Once something is classified as necessary, judgment treats securing it as non-optional. The mind reorganizes itself around obtaining or protecting what it has decided can't be done without. Freedom of action narrows. Flexibility disappears. What started as wanting becomes requiring.

The instruction to "condition yourself" is precise: this isn't a conclusion you reach once. It's a habit of mind built through repeated examination of what desire is calling necessary, and whether that classification is actually warranted. Most things desire labels necessary are things life continues without.

Why This Still Matters

The category of "necessary" expands without supervision. A certain income level. A specific outcome at work. A particular form of recognition. A relationship remaining stable. Each gets quietly classified as necessary by desire, often without examination. Once classified that way, losing any of them feels catastrophic—not because it actually is, but because desire declared it so.

Reviewing what's actually in the necessary category—versus what desire has placed there—often reveals how crowded and arbitrary it has become. Most of the entries were never actually requirements. They were preferences that desire upgraded.

How to Apply This Today

Write down five things you currently treat as necessary for your well-being. Then challenge each: "Would life actually be impossible without this, or have I just been treating it that way?" Most entries won't survive the challenge. The ones that don't belong in the necessary category are precisely where desire has created artificial dependencies.

Remove them from necessary and reclassify them as preferred. Notice what changes—not in the situations, but in your relationship to them. Preferred things that don't arrive are disappointing. Necessary things that don't arrive are catastrophic. The same event; a different classification; a completely different response.

"He who exercises himself against such external impressions is the true athlete in training."

Discourses 3.12.10

What Epictetus Meant

The athletic metaphor does specific work. Training doesn't happen against easy opposition. It happens against exactly the resistance that will be encountered in competition. For judgment, that resistance is the pull of desire toward externals—the impression that this outcome is necessary, that this loss is catastrophic, that this situation requires what can't be commanded.

The training isn't suppression. An athlete doesn't eliminate the opponent; they develop capacity to engage effectively regardless of what the opponent does. Similarly, developing judgment against the pull of misdirected desire isn't about wanting nothing—it's about practicing the correct relationship to desire so that when the pull is strongest, the response is reliable.

Why This Still Matters

Desire as enslaver operates most powerfully in exactly the situations where judgment is already under pressure. High stakes, urgency, emotional intensity—these are when misdirected desire is hardest to see and most costly to follow. Preparation happens in advance, during ordinary situations, so that capacity is present when it matters.

Training the response to desire in low-stakes moments builds the habit that functions under pressure. Without that training, the moment when desire presses hardest is also the moment judgment is least prepared to resist.

How to Apply This Today

Treat ordinary frustrations as training ground. The small desires that don't get met—the delay, the minor inconvenience, the preference overridden—are practice situations for the larger ones. Each time a small desire is examined rather than followed automatically, the capacity builds.

Pick one category of mild desire and practice examining it before acting—for a single week. Not suppressing it—examining it. What's being classified as necessary here? Is that classification warranted? The week's practice isn't valuable for what it produces in the moment. It's valuable for what it builds in the habit.

"Ask not that events should happen as you will, but let your will be that events should happen as they do, and you will have peace."

Discourses 4.7.20

What Epictetus Meant

The closing principle returns to the foundation. Desire as enslaver operates through mismatch: what is wanted and what is available don't align, and desire demands that availability change to match the want. Peace becomes impossible under those terms, because events don't consult desire before occurring.

Reversing the terms ends the mismatch structurally. Not by lowering ambition or accepting whatever happens passively—but by relocating desire to what judgment can actually command. Will operating within its actual domain encounters no resistance from reality. Will extended beyond that domain encounters constant resistance, regardless of how forcefully it's applied.

"You will have peace" is framed as consequence, not promise. It follows structurally from the alignment, the same way disturbance follows structurally from mismatch. The question isn't whether peace is desirable—it's whether desire is placed where peace is possible.

Why This Still Matters

Much of what people call bad luck, unfairness, or difficulty is desire encountering the limits of its actual authority. Not because events are hostile, but because desire has extended itself into territory where its writ doesn't run. The suffering isn't punishment—it's friction from structural mismatch that desire keeps insisting shouldn't exist.

The reorientation doesn't require accepting injustice or abandoning goals. It requires being honest about what the will can actually command. Goals can remain. The demand that circumstances guarantee them has to go.

How to Apply This Today

End this week with one question: "Where am I demanding that events match my wishes, rather than matching my wishes to events?" That location is where desire has extended beyond its authority. It's also where the most persistent frustration lives.

Identify the specific form the demand takes. "This project should have gone differently." "This person should behave the way I need them to." "This situation should be more favorable." Each is desire demanding of events what events can't be commanded to deliver. Restate each as: "This is how it is. Given this, what can I actually do?" The shift from demand to engagement is where peace becomes structurally available.

Chapter 6
Aligning Desire with Control

Desire doesn't need to be eliminated to restore freedom. It needs to be placed correctly. Alignment, not suppression, is the decisive move. Bring desire back within what judgment can command, and its force stabilizes rather than constrains.

Misalignment is what creates dependence. Desire directed outward binds judgment to fortune. Desire redirected inward binds it to choice. The difference is structural. In one case, satisfaction waits on conditions. In the other, it follows from use of what remains available under every circumstance.

The aim isn't wanting less. It's wanting differently. Desire that stays within control no longer presses for outcomes, approval, or confirmation. It attaches itself to intention, consistency, and use of judgment. What follows isn't detachment from life, but independence within it.

This alignment changes how effort is experienced. Action is no longer driven by anticipation of gain or fear of loss. It's governed by commitment to what can be done well regardless of result. Externals no longer receive negotiations from desire—instead, discipline gets reinforced.

Freedom, in this sense, isn't the absence of wanting. It's wanting only what can't be taken away.

"Some things are within our power, while others are not. Within our power are opinion, motivation, desire, aversion, and, in a word, whatever is of our own doing; not within our power are our body, our property, reputation, office, and, in a word, whatever is not of our own doing."

Enchiridion 1

What Epictetus Meant

The boundary is structural, not negotiable. Two categories exist: what operates through your choice, and what doesn't. Opinion, motivation, desire, aversion—these move only when judgment activates them. Body, property, reputation, position—these move according to forces outside command.

The distinction isn't about influence. You can influence many things outside your power. It's about authority. Authority means the final say belongs to you, no conditions required. Desire placed in the first category finds stable ground. Desire placed in the second category builds on terrain that shifts without notice.

Most confusion comes from treating influence as authority. You work hard (influence), so you expect the promotion (authority you don't have). When it doesn't come, disturbance follows—not because you failed, but because desire extended beyond the boundary.

Why This Still Matters

People spend energy securing what can't be secured. Reputation requires others' cooperation. Health requires biology's cooperation. Position requires institutional cooperation. None of these yield to pure will. Yet desire fixes on them as if persistence alone could grant authority.

The exhaustion is predictable. You're trying to command what can only be influenced, and the gap between effort and result feels like personal failure when it's actually structural mismatch.

How to Apply This Today

List what you're currently anxious about. For each item, ask: "Do I have authority here, or just influence?" Authority means you decide, full stop. Influence means you can affect probability but not determine outcome.

Desire placed on authority: sustainable. Desire placed on influence: guaranteed instability. Pull desire back from influence to authority. Notice how much lighter your relationship to the work becomes when you stop asking it to guarantee what it can't.

"Remember that desire demands the attainment of that of which you are desirous; and aversion demands the avoidance of that to which you are averse; that he who fails to obtain the object of his desire is disappointed; and he who incurs the object of his aversion is wretched."

Enchiridion 2

What Epictetus Meant

Desire makes a promise: attainment. Aversion makes a promise: avoidance. The problem isn't desire itself—it's where these promises get applied. Direct desire at what you can't secure, and disappointment follows structurally, not accidentally. Direct aversion at what you can't avoid, and wretchedness follows the same way.

The warning isn't moral. It's mechanical. Desire aimed at externals will disappoint because externals don't obey will. The frequency of disappointment reveals misdirection, not insufficient effort.

Why This Still Matters

People normalize repeated disappointment. "Life is hard. Success is rare. Most things don't work out." True—when desire extends beyond authority. But the conclusion drawn is often "I need to try harder" when the actual issue is "I need to redirect desire."

Track your disappointments over a month. Same pattern recurring? That's not bad luck—it's desire pointed at territory where authority doesn't reach. The disappointment will repeat until placement changes.

How to Apply This Today

Write down three recent disappointments. For each one, identify what you desired and where it falls on the authority/influence spectrum. If it's in the influence category, the disappointment was guaranteed by structure, not by personal failure.

Now reframe: what did you have authority over in that situation? That's where desire should have been placed. Example: Desired the promotion (influence). Had authority over: quality of work, consistency of delivery, skill development. Place desire there. Promotion becomes possible outcome, not required outcome. Disappointment loses structural guarantee.

"Do not seek for things to happen as you wish, but wish for them to happen as they do, and your life will go smoothly."

What Epictetus Meant

Enchiridion 8

The instruction reverses normal operation. Common approach: demand reality conform to preference, then act once it does. Result: constant friction, conditional engagement, perpetual delay waiting for "right conditions."

The reversal: align preference with what's already occurring. Not resignation—strategic repositioning. Desire stops negotiating with reality and starts working within it. "Life goes smoothly" not because obstacles disappear, but because desire stops treating them as obstacles to satisfaction.

Why This Still Matters

Friction exhausts. Not the work itself—the resistance to conditions while doing the work. Someone assigned a project with tight deadline and unclear requirements spends half their energy resisting the conditions ("This shouldn't be this way") and half executing. The resistance doesn't improve conditions. It just adds cost.

Aligned desire encounters the same situation differently: "Given these are the conditions, how do I proceed well?" All energy goes to execution. Same difficulty, half the cost.

How to Apply This Today

Identify one situation where you're fighting conditions while trying to work within them. Notice the split: part of you executing, part of you protesting. The protest doesn't change conditions—it just drains energy that could go to execution.

Practice the shift: "I wish this were different, but it isn't. Given what actually is, what's the best available action?" Not acceptance of outcomes—acceptance of starting conditions. You don't control the conditions. You control what you do within them. Place desire on the second, and the first stops creating friction.

"You can be invincible if you never enter a contest in which victory is not up to you."

What Epictetus Meant

Enchiridion 19

Invincibility comes through selectivity, not through strength. The common approach: enter every contest, try to win everything, build capacity to prevail against all challenges. Result: exposure to defeat in every domain where authority is incomplete.

The alternative: recognize which contests you have authority over (victory up to you) and which you don't (victory dependent on factors outside command). Enter the first. Don't enter the second. Not avoidance—strategic placement of effort where authority actually exists.

"Victory up to you" means: you can secure the outcome through choice and effort alone, no cooperation required. Most contests don't meet this standard. Recognition, advancement, approval—these all require others' participation. You can't be invincible in contests where winning requires cooperation you can't command.

Why This Still Matters

People enter contests they can't win by structure, then experience the inevitable defeat as personal failure. The problem wasn't execution—it was entering a contest where victory wasn't up to them.

Consider someone seeking recognition from a manager who doesn't value their type of work. They do excellent work, it goes unrecognized, they interpret this as failure. But the contest—"gain recognition from this specific person"—was never one where victory was up to them. They needed cooperation they couldn't command. The defeat was structural.

How to Apply This Today

List your current goals. For each one, ask: "Can I secure this through my effort alone, or does it require others' cooperation?" If it requires cooperation, victory isn't up to you. You're in a contest you can't be invincible in.

Reframe the goal: What aspect of this do I have complete authority over? Someone wants book published (requires publisher cooperation—not up to them). What's up to them? Writing the best manuscript they can, submitting it widely, improving craft. Place desire there. Publication becomes possible outcome, not contest they're trying to win. They're invincible in the contest of "wrote well and submitted" regardless of whether publication follows.

"Freedom is secured not by the fulfilling of men's desires, but by the removal of desire."

Discourses 2.16.28

What Epictetus Meant

The common strategy for freedom: fulfill desires. Want X? Get X. Want Y? Get Y. Accumulate enough satisfaction, and freedom follows. The problem: desire is renewable. New wants emerge. The strategy never completes. You're chasing satisfaction that remains perpetually ahead.

The alternative: freedom comes not from fulfilling desire but from removing misdirected desire. Not wanting nothing—wanting correctly. Desire aimed at what you can't command keeps you dependent on conditions cooperating. Remove that desire (redirect it to what you can command), and dependence ends.

This isn't asceticism. It's targeting. Desire remains—it just stops extending where authority doesn't reach.

Why This Still Matters

The fulfillment strategy produces exhaustion. Each desire fulfilled generates new desires. The gap between current state and desired state never closes. You're running on a treadmill that speeds up as you run faster.

The removal strategy produces stability. Desire redirected to what's commandable becomes fulfillable through action alone. The gap closes not by accumulation, but by reorientation.

How to Apply This Today

Track your wants for three days. Write them down as they arise. Then categorize: (1) wants directed at what I can command, (2) wants directed at what I can't command.

Category 1: sustainable. Pursue these. Category 2: structural dependence. These are the ones to remove—not by suppressing the energy, but by redirecting it to Category 1 alternatives.

Example: Want recognition for work (Category 2—requires others). Remove this desire. What's the Category 1 alternative? Want to do work I'm proud of (Category 1—up to me). Redirect the energy there. Recognition becomes bonus, not requirement. Freedom from needing it to feel satisfied.

"When you have assumed these names—good, modest, faithful, sincere—take care not to do anything which will make them fail to apply to you."

Discourses 1.1.23

What Epictetus Meant

The warning addresses the gap between declared identity and demonstrated action. People claim certain qualities—reliable, principled, disciplined—then act in ways that contradict those claims. The instruction: if you've named yourself something, your actions must validate the name. Otherwise, the name is decoration, not description.

This connects directly to desire. What you claim to be should govern what you permit yourself to want. Someone who's declared themselves disciplined can't let desire extend beyond control without invalidating the name. The label imposes constraint—not external constraint, but self-imposed consistency between word and action.

Why This Still Matters

The split between what people say they value and what they actually pursue creates internal contradiction. Someone claims to value integrity but desires recognition badly enough to compromise. Someone claims to value independence but structures desire around external approval. The claimed identity and the actual desire pattern don't match.

This produces two costs: others stop believing the claimed identity (external credibility erosion), and you stop believing it yourself (internal coherence erosion). The second cost is worse. Once you can't trust your own declared commitments, judgment loses its anchor.

How to Apply This Today

Write down three qualities you claim to embody. Now examine your current desires. Do they align with those qualities? Someone who claims to be "independent" but constantly desires others' validation—the desires contradict the claimed identity.

Make the alignment explicit: "If I'm truly [quality], then my desires should be [pattern]." Example: "If I'm truly disciplined, my desires should stay within what I can command." When desires drift outside that pattern, either adjust the desires or drop the claimed identity. The split between the two is where credibility—internal and external—erodes.

"He is free who lives as he wishes, who is subject neither to compulsion, nor hindrance, nor force, whose choices are unhampered, whose desires attain their end, whose aversions do not fall into what they would avoid."

Discourses 4.1.175

What Epictetus Meant

Freedom gets defined through three tests: choices operate without external interference, desires reach their intended target, aversions successfully avoid their object. This sounds like describing someone powerful enough to force reality into compliance. It's actually describing someone who's aligned desire with authority.

Choices unhampered: you're not choosing externals that require permission. Desires attain their end: you're desiring what choice can deliver. Aversions don't encounter their object: you're avoiding only what choice can avoid.

The freedom isn't from dominating circumstances. It's from no longer asking circumstances for what they can't reliably provide. You live as you wish because what you wish for falls within your authority to secure.

Why This Still Matters

Most people define freedom as "getting what I want." The problem: if what you want requires circumstances cooperating, your freedom depends on factors outside your control. You're free only when conditions align favorably.

This definition reverses it: align what you want with what you can command, and freedom becomes independent of conditions. You're free in favorable circumstances and unfavorable ones because satisfaction doesn't require particular circumstances—just the ability to choose well within whatever circumstances exist.

How to Apply This Today

Test your current sense of freedom. When do you feel free, and when constrained? If freedom varies with conditions (good circumstances = free, bad circumstances = constrained), you've placed desire on things outside authority. Your freedom is hostage to cooperation you can't guarantee.

Make the shift: What can I choose regardless of circumstances? That's where desire belongs. When that's secure, circumstances can vary without your freedom varying with them. You're free when you can act well in whatever situation arises, not when situations arrange themselves according to preference.

Practice: Choose one domain where you feel unfree. Identify what you're depending on that's outside your authority. Now identify what's within your authority in that same domain. Shift desire from first to second. Notice whether the feeling of constraint loosens—not because circumstances improved, but because you stopped asking them for what they can't reliably give.

PART IV

ACTION,
ROLE, AND
RESPONSIBILITY

Chapter 7

Playing Your Role Well

Confusion often begins when action is mistaken for identity. A role is taken on, then slowly treated as a definition of the self. Work becomes worth. Authority becomes entitlement. Obligation becomes burden. The line drawn here is hard. Not "who are you?" but "what's required of you, given the position you currently occupy?"

A role, in this view, is functional. It exists to be carried out, not to be admired, defended, or personalized. The moment action is used to confirm status or self-image, judgment weakens. Attention shifts from doing what fits the situation to protecting how one appears within it. This is where resentment, pride, and anxiety quietly enter. The task remains the same, but the inner posture changes—and with it, steadiness is lost.

This chapter addresses that shift. It focuses on how to act fully within social roles—professional, familial, civic—without fastening identity to them. Not withdrawal from responsibility. Removal of the excess weight people add to it. What remains is simpler and more demanding: perform what the role calls for, and nothing more.

"Remember that you are an actor in a play, and the author has given you a part; if a short part, act a short part well; if a long one, act it well; if the author gives you the part of a poor man, act even this part with ability."

Enchiridion 17

What Epictetus Meant

The role contains the standard. What the author assigns—the short part, the subordinate part, the unglamorous part—doesn't determine whether the part can be played well. Only the playing determines that. Complaint against the assigned part treats the author's choice as the problem. But the author's choice isn't subject to revision. What remains is whether the part is carried with ability or abandoned to resentment.

"Even this part" does the work. The poor man's role, the minor role, the role no one wants—these are still roles that can be played well or badly. The standard doesn't change with the status of the assignment. Ability is equally available in the difficult part as in the coveted one.

Why This Still Matters

Resentment toward a role often appears as resentment toward the work itself. People perform the assigned task poorly while mentally occupying a different one. Reliability becomes conditional: full effort for preferred roles, reduced effort for others. Over time this trains inconsistency. When better roles arrive, the habit of partial engagement arrives with them.

The actor who resents the part gives a bad performance. The audience sees it. So do directors, colleagues, family members. The resentment doesn't change the part—it just confirms that the person carrying it has let grievance replace discipline.

How to Apply This Today

Pick one current responsibility that feels beneath the role you believe you should be in. Not one that requires renegotiation—one that is genuinely required and genuinely resented.

Perform it as the author assigned it: fully, with ability, without the commentary that it doesn't match the role you deserve. One week. Notice whether performing it well feels different from performing it resentfully. The task is identical. The difference is entirely in how judgment is oriented toward it.

"Consider at what price you sell your integrity; but please, for God's sake, don't sell it cheap."

Discourses 1.2.11

What Epictetus Meant

The warning addresses compromise within roles. Every position involves pressure to bend standards, hide problems, or prioritize appearance over accuracy. The question isn't whether these pressures exist, but whether they're given authority. Integrity has a price—the role asks what you're willing to trade for approval, advancement, or ease.

The instruction isn't to avoid all compromise. It's to recognize that some prices are too high. When execution requires abandoning what you know to be right, the cost exceeds the value of keeping the role. The boundary is clear: roles are temporary, but how you carry them leaves a permanent mark on judgment.

Why This Still Matters

Career advancement often involves incremental compromises that seem reasonable in isolation. A small deception to meet a deadline. Silence when speaking up might cost standing. Endorsing work you know is flawed. Each choice feels minor, but the pattern trains judgment to negotiate with standards rather than maintain them.

What starts as flexibility becomes habit. The person who compromises easily in small roles continues the pattern in larger ones. The role changes, the authority increases, but the willingness to trade integrity for convenience remains. Result? More responsibility, less trustworthiness.

How to Apply This Today

Notice where your role asks you to compromise. Not impossible ethical dilemmas—everyday pressures to bend accuracy, hide difficulty, or perform agreement you don't feel. Write down one compromise you're currently making. Then ask: "What am I getting for this?" If it's comfort, convenience, or others' approval, you're selling cheap.

The test: Would you make the same choice if you knew it would be made public? If not, the price is wrong.

"Do not seek for things to happen as you wish, but wish for them to happen as they do, and your life will go smoothly."

Enchiridion 8

What Epictetus Meant

Here resistance gets addressed when it's disguised as effort. Wanting events to conform to personal preference introduces friction into action. In the context of roles, this shows up as pushing against the conditions attached to a position instead of working within them. Not advising passivity—eliminating the demand that circumstances justify themselves before action is taken.

By aligning judgment with what's already the case, action becomes direct and unentangled. The role is no longer treated as a negotiation, but as a fact to be met with appropriate conduct.

Why This Still Matters

Frustrations come not from the work itself, but from insisting it should feel different, be easier, or carry more recognition. That insistence adds a second burden on top of the task. Over time, people grow tired not because the role is impossible, but because they're fighting its conditions while trying to perform it.

The pattern shows clearly at work. Someone assigned a task with constraints they dislike—tight timeline, limited resources, unclear authority. They spend energy rehearsing how the situation should be different: "If only I had more time... If only management understood... If only resources were adequate..." Meanwhile, the actual work languishes because effort goes to protest rather than execution.

How to Apply This Today

Routine obligations that provoke irritation reveal the pattern. Instead of rehearsing how things ought to be, notice how much energy is spent resisting what's fixed. Letting the conditions stand as they are clears space to act without the extra weight of protest.

Track one responsibility you resent. Write down: (1) what the role actually requires, (2) what you wish it required. The gap between them is pure resistance, not reality. Drop #2. All your energy goes to #1. Notice how much lighter the work becomes.

"Men are disturbed not by things, but by the views they take of them."

Enchiridion 5

What Epictetus Meant

The correction targets embellishment. A role, taken on its own, consists of specific actions and limits. Disturbance enters when added meanings accumulate—status, injustice, comparison, entitlement. These additions get stripped away. The role is neutral until judgment inflates it.

Once a role is framed as beneath someone, unfair, or defining, resistance replaces function. The work itself hasn't changed; the interpretation has. By identifying judgment as the source of strain, responsibility relocates inward, where adjustment remains possible.

Why This Still Matters

Roles tolerable in practice become exhausting in interpretation. People replay narratives about what their position should signify or how it compares to others'. These stories generate frustration without altering circumstances. Over time, judgment becomes heavier than the role itself, leading to burnout that feels external but is internally produced.

Consider two people with the same deadline-heavy job. One interprets missed deadlines as evidence of impossible demands and incompetent management. Each deadline missed reinforces the narrative: "This place is broken. These expectations are unreasonable. I'm being set up to fail." The other sees missed deadlines as information about where process needs adjustment. Same role, same pressures—completely different internal experience. The difference isn't circumstance. It's interpretation.

How to Apply This Today

Irritation can serve as a signal. Reaction that feels heavier than the task itself requires separation of the concrete demands of the role from the interpretations layered onto it. What remains after that subtraction is usually far more manageable.

Write down what your role actually asks you to do—just the actions, stripped of meaning. Then write what you've been telling yourself it means about you, your worth, or how you're treated. The first list is real. The second is added weight. You can drop the second list without changing anything about the actual work.

"Is it your business to manage public affairs, to get yourself elected to office? Not at all. What is your business then? To manage your own affairs properly."

Discourses 4.10.14

What Epictetus Meant

The distinction separates assigned domain from imagined expansion. Every role has a scope—a defined area where action is both appropriate and effective. Stepping outside that scope doesn't elevate conduct; it weakens it. The given task is left partially undone while energy is diverted to appearances, influence, or authority that doesn't belong to the role.

Discipline means staying proportionate. Judgment keeps action aligned with what the role can rightly support. The question isn't about limiting ambition—it's about recognizing that effectiveness comes from mastery of assigned territory, not from performing roles you don't actually hold.

Why This Still Matters

People often overstep quietly—offering opinions, control, or authority that their position doesn't carry. This creates friction with others and dissatisfaction within. At the same time, essential duties receive less care. Trust erodes externally, focus erodes internally. Overreaching feels like initiative, but often functions as avoidance of the actual work at hand.

Watch for the pattern: someone in a support role who constantly tries to direct strategy. Their actual work—execution—suffers because energy goes to positioning themselves as strategist. They fail at both. The role they have goes undone while they perform a role they don't have. Colleagues notice. Management notices. But the person remains convinced the problem is that their "strategic vision" isn't being recognized, when the actual problem is that their assigned work isn't being completed.

How to Apply This Today

Influence that feels limited often shifts attention toward expanding territory instead of sharpening execution. Notice where effort goes—toward improving what's assigned or toward signaling authority beyond it. That clarifies whether the role is being respected or quietly bypassed.

Before offering input outside your role's scope, ask: "Is my actual work complete?" If not, overreach is avoidance dressed as initiative. Complete your own domain first. Master what's assigned. Then, if expansion is appropriate, it comes from demonstrated competence in your actual role, not from performing roles you wish you had.

"First say to yourself what you would be; and then do what you have to do."

Enchiridion 23

What Epictetus Meant

The sequence matters. Definition precedes execution. Before performing a role, judgment determines the standard it will maintain regardless of circumstance. That standard doesn't come from the role itself—roles vary in difficulty, visibility, and reward. It comes from what you've decided about how you carry responsibility.

This isn't aspiration. It's commitment established in advance. "I would be reliable" means reliability operates whether the task is noticed or not. "I would be thorough" means thoroughness applies to temporary roles and permanent ones equally. The declaration binds action to principle rather than to condition.

Why This Still Matters

A common pattern: treating current responsibilities as placeholders, handled casually because they're not the "real" destination. This mindset trains inconsistency. Even when better roles arrive, the habit of partial engagement follows. What changes is the role. What doesn't change is the relationship to it—conditional execution.

The progression is predictable. Someone in a junior role performs carelessly "because it's beneath them." The work is sloppy, but they tell themselves it doesn't matter because this isn't their permanent position. Promotion comes. The role upgrades. But the habit—the willingness to deliver less than full effort when circumstances don't feel ideal—remains intact. Now they're in the role they wanted, performing it with the same half-hearted approach they practiced in the role they resented. Result? The new role gets handled as poorly as the old one, because the issue was never the role. It was the standard.

How to Apply This Today

Provisional effort tends to show up when a role is treated as temporary or undesired. Holding the same standard of seriousness regardless of preference tests whether discipline depends on circumstance or on judgment.

Choose one task you've been handling carelessly "because it's temporary" or "because it doesn't matter." Execute it as if it were your permanent responsibility and everyone would see the result. Notice what changes in your approach—the attention to detail, the thoroughness, the care. That difference reveals how much discipline you've been making conditional on circumstances being ideal. The gap is where standards have been negotiable. Close it.

"Make the best use of what is in your power, and take the rest as it happens."

Enchiridion 1

What Epictetus Meant

A closing boundary is drawn around attachment. Roles change. They're assigned, modified, expanded, reduced, or ended by factors outside your command. Clinging to a role after it's changed or ended turns memory into identity. Resisting a new role turns necessity into grievance. In both cases, judgment lags behind reality.

What's in your power: how you carry the role while you have it. What isn't: how long it lasts, whether it's recognized, what comes next. Mobility without restlessness gets required—the ability to step out of a role cleanly and step into another without self-dramatization. Roles change. Discipline lies in not letting the self harden around them.

Why This Still Matters

Career shifts, family changes, and social transitions often unsettle people more than loss itself. Identity lingers where function has moved on. This delay produces bitterness toward what ended and suspicion toward what begins. Prolonged instability follows, long after circumstances have already changed.

Think of someone who left a leadership role years ago but still introduces themselves with that old title. Or someone assigned to a new team who spends six months referencing "how we did things" in their previous department. Both are holding identity where it no longer belongs. The clinging prevents clean engagement with what's actually in front of them.

The cost is twofold: they can't properly mourn or appreciate what ended because they won't let it be past, and they can't properly engage what's begun because they keep treating it as temporary or inferior. They're stuck between roles, fully in neither, effective in none.

How to Apply This Today

A role shifts or closes. Attention can be placed on whether resistance comes from loss of function or loss of identity. Identity is optional, and recognizing it shortens the period of disorder.

When a role ends, ask: "What can I no longer do?" (function) vs. "Who am I no longer?" (identity). The first is fact. The second is attachment. Let go of the second, and transition becomes mechanical rather than existential. You're not losing yourself—you're losing a set of tasks. New tasks arrive. Carry them well. That's the pattern. Roles cycle. Standards don't.

Chapter 8

Carrying Duty Without Complaint

Why does obligation so often feel heavier than it is?

Most duties aren't crushing by nature. They become so when complaint is added to them. Complaint isn't a harmless release—it's a failure of judgment. The task remains unchanged, but the mind resists it, argues with it, narrates it as unjust or excessive. That resistance doesn't reduce the burden. It multiplies it.

Endurance here is not passive acceptance, and not moral heroism. It's the refusal to weaken judgment by protesting what must be done. Suffering isn't being praised. The habit of turning necessity into grievance is what gets removed. Duty is then carried plainly, without drama, without added weight.

"Difficulties are what show men's character. Therefore when a difficulty falls upon you, remember that God, like a trainer of wrestlers, has matched you with a rough young man. What for? So that you may become an Olympic conqueror; but it is not accomplished without sweat."

Discourses 1.24.1-2

What Epictetus Meant

The difficulty isn't the problem. It's the material. A wrestler doesn't progress by avoiding strong opponents—the strong opponent is precisely what the training requires. The rough match isn't a sign that something has gone wrong. It's the condition under which capacity is built.

Applied to duty: obligation that feels excessive or unfair isn't evidence of injustice. It's evidence that something is being asked of judgment that judgment can either develop or refuse. The refusal—complaint—doesn't remove the difficulty. It ensures that nothing is gained from it.

"Without sweat" closes the argument. The conqueror requires the difficulty. Remove it, and the achievement disappears with it. Complaint is the attempt to have the prize without the rough young man—which is not how it works.

Why This Still Matters

Difficulty gets treated as error to be corrected rather than as occasion to develop capacity. This reframe costs nothing and changes everything. The same obligation, interpreted as training rather than as imposition, produces different action. Protest softens into engagement. Energy that went to resistance goes to execution.

The shift isn't about enthusiasm. Difficult work can remain difficult. What changes is whether judgment is oriented against the task or inside it.

How to Apply This Today

Identify one duty that currently feels excessive. Not something that requires renegotiation—something that is genuinely required and genuinely resisted. Ask: "What capacity would this build if I stopped treating it as an obstacle and started treating it as the rough young man?" Name that capacity specifically. Then carry the duty with that answer in view.

The reframe doesn't have to feel natural immediately. The wrestler doesn't enjoy every difficult match. What he doesn't do is spend the match narrating how unfair the pairing is.

"With every accident, ask yourself what faculty you have for dealing with it."

Enchiridion 10

What Epictetus Meant

The question redirects attention at the critical moment. When difficulty arrives, the mind's first movement is usually toward the difficulty itself—its unfairness, its inconvenience, its timing. The instruction interrupts that movement and asks instead what's available in response.

Faculty means capacity: the judgment, discipline, patience, or skill that applies to what's occurring. Every difficulty has a corresponding faculty. Hardship calls for endurance. Complexity calls for attention. Provocation calls for restraint. The faculty isn't always comfortable to deploy—but it's always present, which means response is always available.

The question does two things. It removes focus from what can't be changed (the accident itself) and places it on what can be exercised (the response). And it implies that every situation, however difficult, contains the terms of its own resolution—if judgment looks in the right direction.

Why This Still Matters

Complaint addresses the accident: how it shouldn't have occurred, how it was preventable, how it reflects badly on whoever caused it. This is attention aimed entirely at what can't be altered. The faculty question addresses what remains: what's here, what can be deployed, what actually moves the situation forward.

Two people receive the same unexpected setback. One rehearses its causes and the injustice of its timing. The other asks what capacity applies. The task facing both is identical. The direction of attention determines everything that follows.

How to Apply This Today

At the next difficulty—minor or significant—practice asking the question before anything else. Not "why did this happen?" or "who is responsible?" but "what faculty does this call for?"

Write the answer. Endurance? Patience? Precision? Adaptability? Having named the faculty, deploy it. The naming matters: it converts the accident from something that happened to you into something that requires something from you. That shift is where complaint ends and action begins.

"Be for the most part silent, or speak merely what is necessary, and in few words."

Enchiridion 33.1

What Epictetus Meant

The instruction places a boundary around speech that applies directly to how duty is carried. Silence here isn't secrecy or suppression. It's the removal of narration that adds nothing to the work itself. Commentary on effort—explaining, justifying, signaling how difficult things are—shifts attention from execution to self-reference. The work proceeds, but judgment has partially left the task and begun managing its own perception.

"What is necessary" is the standard. If the speech serves the task, it belongs. If it serves to mark effort, invite sympathy, or justify dissatisfaction, it doesn't. The boundary is practical, not punitive. Unnecessary speech drains what execution needs.

Why This Still Matters

Many settings reward narration of difficulty. Announcing fatigue, signaling unfairness, explaining how much effort is being extended—these invite acknowledgment and create momentary solidarity. The habit forms quickly because the reinforcement is real. What also forms: dependence on that acknowledgment, and reduced tolerance for working without it.

When acknowledgment doesn't arrive—and often it doesn't—the result is sharpened resentment. The commentary that was supposed to ease the burden has instead created a new condition: the duty now requires recognition to be bearable. The burden has grown, not shrunk.

How to Apply This Today

For one day, notice how often work is accompanied by commentary—spoken or internal. Fatigue mentioned, unfairness noted, effort indicated. Not to suppress these observations permanently, but to see how much space they occupy.

Then try this: complete one substantial task without narrating it. No announcement of its difficulty before, no summary of its cost after. Notice what changes in the doing. Attention that went to managing perception of the effort goes to the effort itself. Most people find the task takes less out of them when they stop adding the commentary to it.

"What then is it to be properly educated? It is learning to will that things should happen as they do happen, and not to seek after what is given, but only after what is given to you."

Discourses 1.2.5-7

What Epictetus Meant

Education, here, isn't the accumulation of knowledge—it's the alignment of will with what actually occurs. The untrained will presses for what is wished rather than engaging with what is given. The trained will recognizes what is given and works within it, without protest that it should be otherwise.

"What is given to you" is precise. Not what is given to someone else, not what should have been given, not what was given yesterday. What is given to you, now, in this role, under these conditions. That is the material. Endurance without complaint isn't heroic resignation—it's educated will operating correctly. The complaint is evidence that the will hasn't yet learned to take what is given rather than what is wished.

In practice, every obligation involves what is given. The scope of the role, the difficulty of the task, the cooperation or lack of it from others. Will that aligns with what is given proceeds cleanly. Will that demands different terms wastes itself on what isn't available and neglects what is.

Why This Still Matters

The wish for different conditions is one of the most reliable sources of wasted effort. The conditions exist as they are. Acting within them requires no special circumstances—only the decision to stop pressing for what isn't given and start working with what is.

This isn't about lowering standards. It's about locating effort correctly. Someone who keeps insisting on different conditions before engaging fully isn't holding standards high—they're making engagement conditional on circumstances cooperating. That condition rarely gets met, and even when it does, the habit of conditional engagement remains.

How to Apply This Today

Identify one obligation you're currently performing under protest—meeting its requirements while insisting internally that the conditions should be different. More time. Better support. Clearer direction. Fairer distribution.

Now ask: "What is actually given to me here?" List it plainly. What you have, what you can act on, what falls within your part of it. That list is where the educated will works. Everything outside it—the conditions you're wishing were different—is what you're not given. Drop the demand for what you're not given. Work fully with what you are. See what shifts in the execution when the will stops pressing against what isn't available.

"What is a fever? It is a part of life, just as is walking, sailing, and sowing the seed—but a fever is more troublesome. Do you cry out when you sow? That too is a part of life."

Discourses 3.13.21

What Epictetus Meant

The comparison does the work precisely. Walking, sailing, sowing—no one protests these as personal impositions. They're understood as conditions of life, variable in difficulty, accepted as belonging to the situation. Fever carries the same status in terms of its nature, even if not in terms of its comfort.

The question "Do you cry out when you sow?" identifies the inconsistency. Difficulty isn't what triggers complaint—only certain difficulties do. The ones framed as exceptional, unfair, or singular. But that framing is supplied by judgment, not by the nature of the thing. A fever is also a part of life. A difficult duty is also a part of life. Crying out about either doesn't change what it is.

Why This Still Matters

Obligations feel like personal impositions because they're framed that way. The same duty placed on someone else is accepted as part of the role; placed on oneself, it becomes evidence of unfairness. This asymmetry isn't about the duty—it's about the framing.

Remove the framing, and the duty resembles sowing: necessary, sometimes uncomfortable, belonging to the situation without requiring emotional amplification. The work that was generating resentment turns out to be ordinary. It was the narration, not the nature, that made it feel excessive.

How to Apply This Today

Take one obligation that reliably produces complaint. Describe it without the framing: not "I always have to handle this" but "this belongs to the role." Not "this is unfair" but "this is part of the situation." Stripped of personal narrative, describe it as you would describe a task belonging to a role you observe from outside.

Notice what changes. The obligation doesn't shrink, but the weight carried alongside it often does. Most of that weight was narrative, not necessity.

"Duties are universally measured by relations. Is he your father? You are admonished to take care of him, to yield to him in all things, to submit when he is abusive, when he strikes you."

Enchiridion 30

What Epictetus Meant

The relation determines the duty; the duty doesn't require the relation to be pleasant. Epictetus doesn't claim that fathers are always reasonable or that submission is enjoyable. He states simply that the relation carries the obligation. Waiting for the relation to become easier before fulfilling the duty means making obligation contingent on comfort—which is not what obligation means.

"Abusive" and "strikes" aren't chosen casually. Epictetus names the most difficult version of the relation to prevent retreat to an easier case. If the principle holds there, it holds in lesser difficulties. The duty isn't conditioned on the other party's conduct. It follows from what the relation is.

Why This Still Matters

People regularly apply this principle backward: the obligation should match the quality of the relationship. If the colleague is difficult, full effort is withheld. If the manager is unreasonable, compliance becomes grudging. If the family member is demanding, obligation is met with resentment.

But the duty follows the relation, not the performance. Withdrawing full effort because the situation is imperfect doesn't change the relation—it just adds judgment's resistance to what was already difficult.

How to Apply This Today

Identify a relation in which the corresponding duty is currently being met partially or resentfully. Not because the obligation doesn't exist—because the other party's conduct makes full engagement feel unwarranted.

Ask: "Does this relation exist?" If yes, the duty follows from it. Whether the other party is easy or difficult changes the experience of carrying the duty; it doesn't change whether the duty is owed. Carry it as the relation requires, not as the other party's conduct warrants.

"What? Is fever not something natural? How then do you fault it? What does complaining accomplish for your condition?"

Discourses 2.16.41

What Epictetus Meant

The challenge is direct: name what complaint accomplishes. Not rhetorically—actually. Does naming the difficulty reduce it? Does objecting to its existence alter it? If not, complaint isn't release. It's cost without purchase. The condition remains identical with or without protest, but the protest extracts something: attention, energy, steadiness.

"How do you fault it?" targets the underlying assumption that objection is warranted. Natural things—fever, difficulty, obligation, loss—belong to life. Faulting them implies they shouldn't exist. But they do exist, and they will continue to. The protest is aimed at something that isn't listening and won't change. Only the protestor is changed by it.

Why This Still Matters

Complaint is often treated as functional: it releases pressure, marks difficulty, communicates need. Sometimes it does. More often it trains the mind to associate obligation with resistance, so that even manageable duties arrive weighted with protest before they begin.

The result is predictable: reliability erodes. Duties are met late, partially, or with visible friction that contaminates what's around them. The complaint didn't ease the burden—it made the burden harder to carry by training judgment to approach it adversarially.

How to Apply This Today

Before the next complaint—at work, at home, internally—ask the question: "What does this accomplish for my condition?" Answer it honestly.

If the complaint produces information that changes something, it belongs. Sympathy that makes a task bearable has a real cost worth weighing. But if the result is nothing except momentary relief followed by the same task and added resentment, the complaint has failed on its own terms. Notice how often the answer is the third one. That noticing is usually enough to interrupt the reflex.

PART V

DIFFICULTY, LOSS, AND DISTURBANCE

Chapter 9

Holding Steady Under Pressure

Difficulty does not usually announce itself as a test. It arrives as interruption, inconvenience, delay, or disregard. Small things accumulate. Judgment weakens not from a single blow, but from repeated strain applied without correction.

These moments are decisive. Not because they're dramatic, but because they expose how firmly judgment is held under pressure. Losing composure over minor difficulty reveals the same error that fails under major loss: the belief that circumstances should cooperate before steadiness is required. Remove that belief, and difficulty stops being an exception to discipline. It becomes where discipline becomes visible.

The quotes that follow examine how judgment responds when comfort, order, or expectation break down—and why collapse is not caused by difficulty itself, but by the standards carried into it.

"Where is good? In the will. Where is evil? In the will. Where is neither? In things which are independent of the will."

Discourses 2.1.7

What Epictetus Meant

The location is everything. Pressure, inconvenience, loss, delay—none of these are located in the will. They're located in the category of things independent of it. Placing good or evil there means placing it where judgment can't command. The result: stability that depends on circumstances cooperating.

Good located in the will is secured through judgment alone. No circumstance required. No cooperation from events, people, or outcomes. The difficulty can press exactly as hard as it does—and the good remains intact, because it's not stored where difficulty can reach it.

This isn't wordplay. It's the structural answer to why pressure destabilizes. When something external carries the weight of good or evil, anything that threatens that external thing triggers an emergency. The mind treats each difficulty as an attack on good itself. Put good in the will, and difficulty is reduced to what it actually is: a condition requiring response, not a threat to what matters most.

Why This Still Matters

Pressure feels disproportionate when it touches something classified as essential. The mild frustration that should require mild response instead triggers alarm—because behind it sits something that's been placed in the wrong category. Audit what's been classified as good. If it's external, every difficulty in that domain will feel like a crisis, regardless of actual severity.

How to Apply This Today

Identify your most recent strong reaction to a difficulty. Not the largest difficulty of your life—the most recent one that produced a response bigger than the situation warranted. Ask: what was located there that made the threat feel significant? If the answer is external—reputation, outcome, others' approval—you've found where good has been misclassified. Relocate it. The same difficulty, with good in the will, requires no emergency.

"It is not he who gives abuse or blows who affronts you, but the view you take of these things as insulting."

Discourses 1.25.1

What Epictetus Meant

The affront is manufactured. Not by the event, not by the person delivering the difficulty, but by the interpretation applied to it. The blow lands on the body. The insult lands on nothing—unless judgment agrees that an insult has occurred and confirms it.

This removes the source of pressure from the person or event and places it where it actually originates: in the view taken. The person who abuses doesn't possess the power to affront. That power is granted or withheld by the one receiving. Grant it, and the affront exists. Withhold it, and it doesn't—regardless of what was said or done.

The instruction isn't to pretend nothing happened. The event occurred. What doesn't need to occur is the classification of that event as affronting. That classification is the work of judgment, and judgment can revise it.

Why This Still Matters

Pressure multiplies fastest through interpretation. A remark, a dismissal, a small slight—these arrive once. The interpretation rehearses them. The mind replays the scene, revises the affront upward, imagines responses, assigns motives. The original difficulty was brief. The amplification is extended. And the amplification, unlike the event, is entirely produced from the inside.

How to Apply This Today

Take one recent moment where a remark or action from another person produced lasting irritation—lingering past the moment itself. Separate what actually occurred from what you concluded about it. The event: a specific thing that was said or done. The interpretation: what you decided it meant about you, about them, about the relationship.

The event is fixed. The interpretation was constructed. A constructed interpretation can be revised. Ask: what's the least loaded interpretation that still accounts for
the facts? Often it's more accurate than the one that's been generating irritation.
Adopt it provisionally and notice whether the lingering pressure reduces.

**"You ought to exercise yourself in small things, and thence pass on to those
of greater importance."**

Discourses 3.12.1

What Epictetus Meant

Capacity doesn't appear on demand. It's built incrementally, from small exercises
toward larger ones. Expecting composure under significant difficulty without having practiced composure under minor difficulty is expecting a result without the
preparation that produces it.

Small things aren't trivial because the stakes are low. They're valuable precisely
because they're the training ground. The delay, the minor irritation, the small interruption—these are the weights with which endurance is built. Dismiss them, and
the capacity they could have developed goes unbuilt. Arrive at larger difficulty with
that gap, and composure fails—not from weakness, but from missing preparation.

Why This Still Matters

Collapse under pressure rarely arrives without warning. It's rehearsed first in smaller
situations where it was tolerated as inconsequential. Frequent irritation over minor
things trains the response pattern that will appear under major pressure. This isn't
abstract—it's behavioral. Each time a small difficulty produces a disproportionate
response, that response is being reinforced as the default. The habit forms in the
small exercises, whether or not they're recognized as exercises.

How to Apply This Today

Identify three minor difficulties that reliably produce irritation: a slow process, a recurring interruption, a repeated small frustration. These aren't the problems to solve. They're the training ground.

For one week, treat each as an exercise in composure rather than an annoyance to survive. Not suppressing the irritation—noticing it, holding steady, letting it pass without amplification. The week won't transform composure under major difficulty. It will build the substrate from which that composure grows. Athletes don't train only on game day.

"Never shun being seen doing what clear judgment approves, even if the world should misunderstand it."

Enchiridion 35

What Epictetus Meant

Pressure frequently arrives in social form: the awareness that others are observing, evaluating, or disapproving. Judgment that is clear about what ought to be done faces a second test—whether that clarity survives when others seem to see it differently. Epictetus refuses the softening. If judgment has examined the matter and arrived at a sound conclusion, the presence of others who disagree or misread it doesn't alter the conclusion.

"Even if the world should misunderstand" is precise. Misunderstanding from others doesn't equal error in judgment. These are separate categories. Allowing others' misunderstanding to revise a sound judgment is capitulation dressed as responsiveness.

Why This Still Matters

Social pressure operates by offering an alternative standard: not what judgment concludes, but what others conclude. When these diverge under pressure, many people revise toward the social reading. It feels like responsiveness. It operates as abandonment of judgment.

The capacity to act on clear judgment regardless of social reading isn't rigidity—it's the capacity to maintain the standard that was established before pressure arrived. Without it, every difficult situation becomes a referendum on whether judgment or others' perception will govern response.

How to Apply This Today

Recall one instance where you revised a judgment not because new information arrived but because others' disapproval made the original position uncomfortable. The decision may have been defensible either way—that's not the point. The question is what moved you: the merits, or the pressure?

Next time judgment arrives at a clear conclusion and social pressure pushes against it, ask: "Is there new information here, or only disagreement?" New information warrants revision. Disagreement alone doesn't. Hold the distinction, and the social pressure loses its authority over what judgment has already examined.

"What are exile and imprisonment and bonds and death and dishonor? These things befall the good and bad alike. They are then not good nor evil."

Discourses 3.18.1

What Epictetus Meant

The argument is structural. Whatever befalls good and bad people indiscriminately can't be classified as good or evil in itself. It's neutral—belonging to the category of things that happen, not the category of things that carry inherent value or harm. Exile strikes the just and unjust. Illness doesn't reserve itself for the corrupt. Death belongs to everyone without exception. Their distribution alone disqualifies them from bearing the weight of good or evil.

What this does to difficulty: it removes the moral catastrophe. A difficult circumstance isn't evidence of failure, isn't punishment, isn't inherently bad. It's something that happens—requiring response, not requiring collapse. The collapse follows from the misclassification, not from the thing itself.

Why This Still Matters

Difficulty feels catastrophic when it's been preloaded with moral weight. Failure means something about worth. Setback means something about trajectory. Loss means something about what was deserved. Strip the moral loading, and what remains is a situation requiring action. That's still hard—but it's a different kind of hard. Manageable rather than devastating.

The same event, classified correctly, produces a different response. Not because the situation changed, but because the judgment applied to it did.

How to Apply This Today

Take a current difficulty and strip it of moral narrative. Not "this means I've failed" but "this is what's occurring." Not "this shouldn't be happening to me" but "this is the situation." Describe it as you would describe weather: conditions present, response required, no inherent verdict on the person experiencing it.

Write it down that way. The stripped description often reveals how much of the difficulty was in the moral overlay rather than in the situation itself. The conditions remain. The verdict was added. The verdict can be removed.

"The characteristic of a vulgar person is that he never expects benefit or harm from himself, but from externals."

Enchiridion 48

What Epictetus Meant

The definition is unflattering but precise. Vulgarity here isn't about manners—it's about where benefit and harm are expected to originate. Someone who locates both in externals has organized their entire relationship to difficulty around what they can't command. Every good thing depends on circumstances cooperating. Every harmful thing depends on circumstances not cooperating. That arrangement guarantees a mind perpetually managed by what happens outside it.

The reverse: expecting benefit and harm from yourself places both where judgment actually has authority. Benefit comes from using that authority well. Harm comes from neglecting or misusing it. Difficulty stops being the source of harm—it's merely the condition within which judgment operates better or worse.

Why This Still Matters

Pressure operates most effectively on people who have placed benefit and harm in external locations. Each difficulty threatens something classified as essential. The threat feels real because the classification made it so. Move the classification inward, and the same difficulty stops threatening what matters. It threatens only the external conditions—which were never the location of the relevant benefit anyway.

How to Apply This Today

Scan a week of recent reactions to difficulty. For each one, identify: where was the harm located? In what was threatened, lost, or inconvenienced? Or in how judgment responded to it?

If harm was located externally in every case, benefit is also located there—and that arrangement guarantees fragility. Begin relocating. What was the judgment in each situation? Did it respond with clarity and steadiness? If yes, no real harm occurred, regardless of what the situation produced. If no, harm occurred at the source—in judgment's response—not in the external event.

"Show me a man who though sick is happy, though in danger is happy, though dying is happy, though condemned and disgraced is happy."

Discourses 4.6.26

What Epictetus Meant

The demand is extreme deliberately. Sick, in danger, dying, condemned—these aren't inconveniences. Epictetus selects the worst cases to establish where the standard actually sits. Composure that holds only under mild difficulty isn't composure—it's ordinary functioning. The real question is where the floor is: how deep can difficulty go before judgment fails?

The answer he's pointing toward: happiness that depends on the absence of these conditions isn't happiness at all. It's conditional comfort. Happiness that persists through them is the product of judgment correctly oriented—with good located in the will, with harm stripped of its moral loading, with the source of benefit and harm correctly identified.

This isn't asked of readers as an immediate achievement. It's presented as the direction—the standard against which progress is measured. Composure under minor difficulty is progress toward this. Loss of composure under minor difficulty is movement away from it.

Why This Still Matters

The everyday pressures—delays, dismissals, minor failures, small frustrations—are the same in kind as the larger ones, only smaller in scale. How they're handled reveals the orientation that would appear under larger pressure. Someone who loses composure over a delayed flight is practicing for how they'll respond to worse. That's not a comfortable conclusion. It's a useful one.

How to Apply This Today

Take the pressures of the current week and ask: if this is where composure is tested, what standard does my response reflect? Not as self-criticism—as calibration.

Then work backward: what's the smallest difficulty this week that produced a response bigger than it warranted? That gap—between the difficulty and the response—is where the work lives. Close it in the small situation, and the same capacity is available when the situation is larger. The man who is happy though dying didn't develop that capacity at the moment of dying. He developed it in every smaller moment where he could have collapsed and didn't.

Chapter 10

Independence from Praise and Blame

Praise and blame appear to be opposites, but they work in the same way. Both place judgment outside the agent. Approval invites dependence; criticism invites defense. In each case, attention shifts away from what is being done and toward how it is being received.

That shift is a loss of independence. Action begins to follow reaction. Standards rise or fall based on response rather than reason. Over time, the desire to be approved and the fear of being judged quietly replace internal measure. What looked like sensitivity or professionalism becomes a form of exposure.

Freedom from praise and blame isn't indifference. It's the recovery of judgment from the hands of whoever happens to be responding.

"If you seek to please others, you will seek to please in the wrong way."

Enchiridion 23

What Epictetus Meant

The error is structural, not motivational. Seeking to please orients judgment outward—toward what will be received well rather than toward what is correct. Once that orientation takes hold, the standard shifts with each audience. What pleased the last group may not please the next. What worked yesterday gets revised for today. The agent is no longer evaluating action by its own merit but by its anticipated reception.

"In the wrong way" names the consequence. Pleasing oriented toward reception rather than toward what is right produces distorted conduct. Not because audiences are always wrong—sometimes their approval tracks correctness—but their approval isn't the reason conduct is correct. Allowing it to become the reason corrupts the standard.

Think of someone who adjusts their position in a meeting based on who's nodding. The position isn't determined by what they've examined and concluded—it's determined by where warmth is coming from. They leave the meeting having said whatever maintained approval, which may or may not correspond to what they actually think. The approval was secured. The judgment was abandoned to secure it.

Why This Still Matters

Approval-seeking operates invisibly because it mimics responsiveness. Adjusting to an audience looks like communication. Softening a position looks like openness. Only the motive distinguishes accommodation from genuine engagement. When the motive is approval, what's called responsiveness is actually surrender of the standard.

How to Apply This Today

Before a conversation where approval matters—a presentation, a difficult discussion, a high-stakes interaction—write down what you actually think about the subject. After the conversation, compare what you said to what you wrote. The gap reveals where approval-seeking reshaped what was expressed.

Do this three times in one week. The pattern will show which contexts pull judgment outward most reliably. Those are where the work is.

"If anyone tells you that a certain person speaks ill of you, do not make excuses about what is said of you, but answer: 'He was ignorant of my other faults, else he would not have mentioned only these.'"

Enchiridion 33.9

What Epictetus Meant

The response reframes blame entirely. Defensiveness accepts the critic's frame: the criticism is being contested because it matters. This response does something different—it treats the criticism as incomplete rather than inaccurate. A full account would have more to say. Neither confirming nor disputing the specific criticism, it removes the critic's authority to define the terms of the exchange.

This isn't sarcasm. It's the practical result of having separated self-assessment from others' assessment. Someone whose standards rest on their own examined judgment doesn't need to contest blame. Blame is data—possibly useful, possibly not—but it doesn't determine standing. Defense becomes necessary only when standing is located in others' opinion.

Why This Still Matters

Defense is expensive. It requires engaging with the criticism's frame, producing evidence within that frame, and waiting for a verdict within that frame. The critic has already set the terms. Even a successful defense leaves judgment shaped by what was contested rather than by what was examined independently.

Those who don't need to defend aren't indifferent to accuracy. They examine criticism privately, take what's useful, and don't perform the examination for the critic's benefit. That privacy preserves independence in a way that public defense never can.

How to Apply This Today

The next time criticism arrives—public or private—practice a one-breath delay before responding. In that breath, ask: "Am I about to defend myself to change the critic's mind, or because their view of me is currently determining how I feel about myself?"

If the second, the defense is aimed at restoring standing that's been located in the wrong place. Don't dispute the criticism. Examine it privately. Take what's accurate. Discard what isn't. The critic's view changes or it doesn't—either way, it doesn't have to be the unit of measure.

"Never call yourself a philosopher, nor talk a great deal among the unlearned about your principles, but act on your principles."

Enchiridion 46

What Epictetus Meant

The trap being named is subtler than it appears. Talking about principles to others invites their response—approval or challenge. Once that invitation is issued, judgment begins to bend toward the audience. Principles get softened for easier reception, sharpened for better effect, or adjusted to avoid conflict. What began as expression of examined position becomes performance of it for an audience whose approval is now at stake.

Acting on principles requires no audience. The conduct itself carries the standard. No one needs to observe it, assess it, or confirm it. By removing the performance, the point at which others' response gains leverage is also removed.

Why This Still Matters

Identity often gets announced before it's established. People describe their values and commitments in advance—sometimes as substitute for acting on them, sometimes because the announcement invites acknowledgment the action itself wouldn't guarantee. Each announcement creates a new relationship with audience response: the values are now held partly in others' hands.

Those who act on principles without announcing them are harder to flatter and harder to shame. No declared position exists to praise into overclaiming or criticize into retreat. The conduct is what it is, independent of response.

How to Apply This Today

For two weeks, stop announcing what you value and start acting on it without commentary. When you would normally signal your principles—in conversation, in writing, in how you explain a decision—let the action stand without the explanation.

Notice two things: whether the action changes when the announcement is removed (which reveals whether the announcement was doing work the action couldn't), and whether others' response changes when there's no declared position to respond to.

"Seek not the good in external things; seek it in yourself."

Discourses 3.20.9

What Epictetus Meant

Praise is external. It belongs to others, arrives unpredictably, and can't be commanded. Locating good there means locating good where it fluctuates with others' moods, attention, and standards—none of which track what was actually done or how well judgment was applied.

Good located in the self means good in what judgment actually commands: the care taken, the honesty maintained, the standard held regardless of response. Once located there, praise becomes incidental—pleasant when it arrives, irrelevant when it doesn't. Blame becomes information to be examined—useful when accurate, dismissible when not. Neither carries authority over standing, because standing isn't stored where they can reach it.

Why This Still Matters

The volatility many people experience around evaluation—the lift from approval, the drop from criticism—isn't sensitivity. It's evidence that good has been located externally. Confidence that rises and falls with others' responses isn't confidence. It's a barometer for others' moods, dressed as self-assessment.

Once good is relocated inward, the volatility doesn't disappear immediately—the habit runs deep. But each instance where approval doesn't lift and blame doesn't deflate is evidence that the relocation is taking hold.

How to Apply This Today

Track your confidence for one week—not in a journal, just notice it. When it rises, ask what caused it. When it falls, ask the same. How much of the movement traces to what you did, and how much to how others responded?

When the second category dominates, good is stored externally. Begin the relocation: after each piece of work, assess it yourself before looking for response. Write one sentence: "This is what I think of what I did." Then check for response if you want. Over time, the self-assessment comes first and the external response loses its power to rewrite it.

"When you are going to meet anyone, especially one of those who are in great repute, propose to yourself the question: What would Socrates or Zeno have done in this case?"

Enchiridion 33.12

What Epictetus Meant

The instruction removes the social moment from the grip of immediate reaction. Instead of walking into an encounter governed by what approval is available or what criticism might come, judgment orients to a standard that exists independently of the person being met. Socrates and Zeno aren't available to approve or disapprove—their standard is internal, fixed, and immune to the social pressure of the room.

High-status encounters trigger approval-seeking most reliably. The question redirects attention from "how will I be received?" to "what would someone whose judgment I actually respect do here?" That standard doesn't fluctuate with the other person's response.

Why This Still Matters

Independence from praise and blame is hardest to maintain when the person distributing them carries weight with you. A superior's approval, a mentor's criticism, a respected peer's assessment—these feel different. The principle hasn't changed; the pressure is just higher.

Having a standard that exists independently of the room gives judgment somewhere to orient that doesn't shift with the dynamics of the encounter. "What would Socrates do?" isn't about mimicry. It's about recovering a fixed reference point when the room is applying pressure to abandon one.

How to Apply This Today

Before your next high-stakes social encounter, decide in advance whose standard you'll orient toward. Not Socrates specifically—anyone whose judgment you respect and who wouldn't adjust their conduct based on who's in the room.

Carry that standard in. When you feel the pull toward approval—softening a position, performing agreement, avoiding a necessary observation—ask what your chosen standard would do. Not as a rule to follow mechanically, but as a fixed point that prevents the room's pressure from becoming the only reference available.

"If you wish to be good, first believe that you are bad."

Discourses 2.11.1

What Epictetus Meant

The instruction cuts against praise at its most insidious point. Approval tends to confirm the current state—to suggest that what is being done is sufficient, that the standard is being met, that no correction is required. Believing you are bad, in this sense, isn't self-abasement. It's refusal to let praise settle the question of where you actually stand.

Someone who believes they are good has handed the standard to whoever is approving. Someone who believes there is still ground to cover retains the standard internally, because no amount of external approval resolves whether what is being done is actually as good as it can be. Blame, correspondingly, loses its power to destabilize—because the person already holds a more demanding internal assessment than the critic is likely to offer.

Why This Still Matters

Praise is most dangerous when it arrives in place of improvement. Consistent approval trains the feedback loop backward: instead of good conduct attracting honest assessment, honest assessment gets filtered to preserve approval. The approved person and the good person diverge—and the divergence is invisible from inside, because the external signal remains positive.

Maintaining the internal question—"is this actually good, or just approved?"—keeps judgment active where praise would put it to sleep.

How to Apply This Today

After receiving approval for something—a compliment, positive feedback, recognition—ask one question before accepting it as settled: "Is this actually as good as I can do, or is it as good as was expected?"

Not false modesty. Maintenance of the standard that praise threatens to retire. "It could be better" means the approval is acknowledged but not allowed to close the inquiry. "No, this is genuinely as good as I can do right now" means accept it without drama—and know that judgment made that determination, not the person offering the praise.

PART VI

STOIC PRACTICE
AS DAILY TRAINING

Chapter 11

Training Attention and Judgment

Understanding a rule does not make it operative. There's a sharp line between knowing what is correct and being able to hold it under strain. Without training, judgment fails at the first point of pressure—not because the rule was unclear, but because attention was never stabilized.

This chapter turns from explanation to use. Attention is a faculty that weakens or strengthens through repetition. Judgment isn't assumed to be available on demand. It must be kept ready. Training consists in correction applied consistently, especially in small moments that seem insignificant.

Discipline here is maintenance rather than insight. Not improvement through intensity, but steadiness through repetition. What is practiced daily is what appears under pressure. Everything else remains theoretical.

"If you wish to improve, be content to be thought foolish and stupid with respect to externals."

Enchiridion 13

What Epictetus Meant

Progress carries a social cost. Attention directed toward what actually requires judgment—conduct, assent, response—is attention withdrawn from the performance of competence. Tracking opinions, demonstrating knowledge, managing impressions: these consume the same attention that training requires. Choosing to invest it in training means accepting that the performance side will suffer.

"Content to be thought foolish" is precise. It doesn't require being foolish—it requires tolerating the appearance of it in order to direct attention where it actually belongs. Most people pay this cost unconsciously, optimizing for appearance rather than for capacity, without noticing the trade.

The trade is real. Attention is finite. Every unit spent managing how one appears is a unit unavailable for the work of maintaining judgment. Improvement requires the willingness to let that performance slide.

Why This Still Matters

Attention pulled toward impression management is attention that can't be applied to correction. The habit forms quietly: opinion offered where no opinion was needed, appearance tracked instead of conduct examined, energy spent on how things seem rather than on what they are. The result isn't dramatic failure—it's steady dilution of the faculty that discipline depends on.

How to Apply This Today

For one day, track how many times you form or express an opinion about something that doesn't actually require your judgment—news, others' decisions, matters outside your role. Each one is attention diverted.

Then track separately how many times you return attention to what actually depends on you—your conduct, your response, your standard. The ratio reveals what's actually being trained. Adjust it deliberately for one week and notice what changes in the quality of judgment when it's needed.

"First say to yourself what you would be; then do accordingly."

Discourses 3.23.1

What Epictetus Meant

The sequence is the discipline. Declaration precedes action—not as aspiration, but as the setting of a standard against which action will be measured. Without the declaration, action floats: it follows mood, circumstance, or the path of least resistance. With it, there's a fixed point to return to when attention drifts.

This isn't goal-setting. It's the daily practice of re-establishing what standard applies before engaging with whatever the day brings. The question "what would I be?" asked at the start of a specific task, interaction, or period of work anchors attention before pressure arrives. Pressure that finds attention already anchored is easier to hold against than pressure that finds attention scattered.

Why This Still Matters

Judgment rarely collapses suddenly. It drifts. The standard was present in principle, but attention never anchored to it before the situation demanded it. By the time a decision is required, attention is already downstream—tracking circumstances, reactions, and outcomes rather than the fixed point from which a clean judgment could be made.

Declaring the standard in advance is the corrective. It gives attention somewhere specific to return to when it drifts, which it will.

How to Apply This Today

Before any significant task or interaction this week, write one sentence: "In this, I would be [quality]." Not a goal—a standard. Reliable. Clear. Patient. Whatever fits.

Then, when attention drifts during that task—toward how it's being received, toward what comes next, toward irritation with conditions—return to the sentence. It functions as an anchor. The return itself is the training. Each time attention is brought back, the faculty strengthens.

"Practice the things which you think you are not able to do."

Discourses 3.12.5

What Epictetus Meant

Capacity doesn't reveal itself through assessment. It develops through use—specifically through use in areas where it's currently absent. Knowing you're impatient and reasoning about impatience produces nothing. Practicing patience in situations that trigger impatience does. The gap between understanding and capacity is closed only by putting attention into the thing that's currently missing.

"Think you are not able to do" names the precise location of the work. Comfort zones produce comfort; they don't produce new capacity. Training that stays within what's already established merely maintains the existing level. Expansion requires working in the area of actual limitation.

Why This Still Matters

Improvement plans focus on strengths and interests, which is the opposite of what this instruction requires. The capacity that fails under pressure is rarely the one being refined in training. It's the one being avoided because it's uncomfortable to work with. That avoidance ensures it remains unavailable when needed.

The pattern is predictable: careful in low-stakes situations, reactive in high-stakes ones. The gap exists because low-stakes training stays comfortable. High-stakes situations call on capacity that was never practiced at the level it's now being demanded.

How to Apply This Today

Identify one specific capacity that you know fails under pressure. Not a weakness in general—a precise behavior: patient listening when interrupted, steady tone when challenged, clear decision when options are uncomfortable.

For two weeks, seek out situations where that specific capacity is tested—deliberately, at a manageable level. Not crisis-level pressure. Situations that trigger the pattern without overwhelming it. Every instance is a training session. The capacity being avoided is the capacity that needs the most repetition.

"Know first who you are; and then adorn yourself accordingly."

Discourses 3.1.25

What Epictetus Meant

Adornment without identity is performance. The instruction targets the habit of acquiring practices, rules, and frameworks—adorning judgment with the appearance of discipline—while the underlying question of who is doing the judging remains unexamined. Without knowing what you are, training has no stable target. You practice responses without a self to anchor them to.

"Know first" is a sequencing requirement. Identity precedes practice. This doesn't mean an extended philosophical project before any action is taken. It means: in the specific situation, before adding a technique or rule, ask what kind of person would be appropriate here—and whether that's actually you, or a performance of what you think discipline looks like.

Why This Still Matters

Training gets accumulated as collection: techniques added to existing confusion rather than as expression of something already understood. The result is inconsistency—a collection of practices that produce different outputs depending on which one happens to be activated in a given moment. What looks like discipline from the outside is a set of acquired responses with no coherent center.

Discipline that knows itself is different. It produces the same output under different conditions because it isn't drawing on a collection—it's drawing on something consistent.

How to Apply This Today

Look at your current practices for maintaining judgment: anything you do deliberately to keep attention stable. Now ask honestly: do these practices express who you've determined yourself to be, or are they borrowed frameworks you haven't yet fully occupied?

There's no wrong answer. The point is to notice the difference. Practices that express something real about your actual standard tend to hold under pressure. Borrowed frameworks tend to dissolve exactly when they're needed most. Identify which of your current practices belong to which category. Invest more in the first.

"If you would improve, lay aside such reasonings as these: 'If I neglect my affairs, I shall not have the means of living.' For it is better to die of hunger, having lived without grief and without fear, than to live with a troubled spirit, amid abundance."

Discourses 4.9.3

What Epictetus Meant

The instruction identifies the reasoning that blocks training. The justification "I can't attend to judgment because practical concerns require attention first" keeps attention permanently occupied with externals. The claim is that improvement must wait until circumstances are arranged correctly. But circumstances never arrange themselves completely. The wait is indefinite.

Epictetus frames the alternative starkly: better to lack abundance and hold judgment intact than to have abundance with a troubled spirit. The practical concern isn't being dismissed—it's being weighed against the cost of the disturbance it produces when allowed to dominate attention. That cost is often higher than the benefit it protects.

What the instruction trains is prioritization. Attention given first to what depends on judgment, then to what can be managed. Not the reverse, which is the default.

Why This Still Matters

The "practical first" argument is self-renewing. Once practical matters receive first claim on attention, there's always another one. Each day generates new demands. Judgment receives whatever remains, which is usually nothing. The troubled spirit appears not as a one-time cost but as a permanent condition—visible to everyone except the person experiencing it as baseline.

The choice being described is available every day: attend to what can actually be held, or attend to what cannot be fully controlled and accept the instability that follows.

How to Apply This Today

List what received your attention first this morning. Then list what requires your judgment most today. How much overlap exists between the two lists?

When they diverge—practical demands first, judgment left for later—the default is operating. Reverse the sequence for one week: before handling external demands, spend ten minutes attending to where judgment is currently settled or unsettled. That attention doesn't replace practical action. It precedes it, so that practical action is taken from a steadier base.

"Confine yourself to the present."

Discourses 3.11.2

What Epictetus Meant

Attention that ranges across past and future has left the only location where judgment operates: now. Reviewing what went wrong, anticipating what might go wrong, managing outcomes not yet arrived—all of this is real mental activity, but none of it is where choice exists. Choice exists only in what can be acted on presently. Attention confined to the present is attention located where it can actually be used.

This isn't about ignoring past or future. Planning belongs to the present. Reflection that informs current judgment belongs to the present. What doesn't belong is attention absorbed into what's over or not yet here, at the cost of clarity about what's immediately available for action.

Why This Still Matters

Distracted attention isn't only pulled toward messages and interruptions. It's pulled toward what happened and what might happen—internal noise that feels like thinking but is often rehearsal without action. Plans get reviewed without being revised. Regrets get replayed without producing correction. Both occupy attention without returning anything that improves judgment in the moment that's actually present.

How to Apply This Today

During any task today that requires attention, notice when thinking leaves the present. Not to stop it—to observe where it goes. Anticipation of how the task will be received. Review of something related that went poorly before. Comparison with how the task would look if circumstances were different.

Each departure is a moment when attention is consuming itself without producing anything available for action. The return—simply noticing the departure and coming back—is the training. It doesn't require suppressing the thought. It requires noticing that it took attention somewhere judgment can't follow, and bringing attention back.

"Practice yourself in little things, and thence proceed to greater."

Discourses 1.18.20

What Epictetus Meant

Scale is not the variable. The pattern of response is the variable. What fails under large pressure has already been failing under small pressure—it was just tolerated there because the stakes seemed low. Epictetus removes the distinction. The small thing is the place where the pattern gets established. Get it right at small scale, and it holds at large scale. Tolerate it at small scale, and it will fail at large scale, reliably.

"Thence proceed to greater" requires the small work to be real—not token practice, but actual application of the same standard that would be required if the stakes were high. What separates how a small irritation is handled from how a significant one is handled is what's been practiced versus what's been assumed.

Why This Still Matters

Failures under pressure are explained as exceptions: exceptional circumstances, exceptional stress, exceptional difficulty. Sometimes true. More often, the pattern was present in small form throughout the preceding weeks. The exception revealed a habit, not an aberration.

Correcting at small scale is available every day. Most of it gets passed over because the consequences seem negligible. They are—in that moment. Cumulatively, each small tolerance sets the standard that appears when the stakes rise.

How to Apply This Today

Identify the pattern most likely to fail when pressure increases. Not a character flaw—a specific behavior: allowing distraction when focusing matters, letting irritation show when composure is needed, making a decision before attention is settled.

For one week, correct that specific behavior every time it appears—regardless of how small the situation. Not intensely. Just consistently. The minor interruption handled with the same standard as the significant one. The small irritation met with the same steadiness as the large one. Consistency at small scale is what builds the capacity that holds at large scale.

Chapter 12

Living as a Disciplined Agent

What does it mean to live as someone whose judgment can be relied on?

Not a peak state or a finished character. A condition maintained through consistency. A disciplined agent isn't someone who never falters, but someone whose standards don't change with mood, pressure, or response. Action remains aligned even when attention is strained.

This closing chapter brings the parts together without summary or reassurance. The focus is integration: carrying the same measure into work, difficulty, praise, blame, and routine. Discipline isn't intensity, and not self-control displayed at moments of crisis. It's the quiet persistence of judgment that holds across situations, because it has been practiced there already.

"Never esteem anything as of advantage to you that will make you break your word or lose your self-respect."

Enchiridion 12

What Epictetus Meant

The instruction sets the floor. Before any other standard can hold, this one does: no advantage—practical, social, financial, reputational—justifies breaking the agreement judgment has made with itself. Once advantage can override that agreement, judgment is no longer setting the terms. Advantage is.

"Break your word" and "lose your self-respect" are paired deliberately. The first is the external breach—what others observe. The second is the internal one—what the agent knows about themselves regardless of what others see. The concern is less with the visible failure than with the invisible one: the moment when judgment agrees that this advantage is worth the breach. That agreement is where integrated discipline either holds or dissolves.

The temptation is rarely dramatic. Small adjustments accumulate—each one modest, each one justified—and amount to the same breach, made gradually enough that no single step feels like the decision. Discipline here doesn't hold at the visible moments. It holds at all the invisible ones that lead there.

Why This Still Matters

Every practical compromise has a justification. The justification is real—advantages are real, costs are real. What gets refused is the reasoning that places advantage above the standard. Not because advantages don't matter, but because once judgment accepts that reasoning once, it becomes available again. The exception trains the next exception.

How to Apply This Today

Identify one advantage you're currently considering that requires bending something you've committed to—a standard, an agreement, a principle. Name the bend explicitly. Not the justification for it—the actual thing that would be compromised.

Then ask: what gets trained if you accept this? Not just this time—what becomes available to judgment the next time a similar advantage appears? That question is usually more honest about the real cost than the immediate justification.

"Seek to be worthy of esteem, not merely esteemed."

Discourses 2.22.29

What Epictetus Meant

Worthiness is internal; esteem is external. Being worthy of esteem means the standard exists independently of whether anyone is offering it. Being merely esteemed means the standard is located in others' assessment—present when they approve, absent when they don't.

The distinction matters for integration because esteem varies. Contexts change, audiences change, reception changes. A standard anchored in worthiness stays constant across those variations. One anchored in esteem inherits all their volatility. Integrated discipline requires the first. The second produces consistent behavior only in front of audiences likely to reward it.

Why This Still Matters

Reputation and character diverge precisely when the reliable audience is absent. Decisions made when no one who matters would notice the outcome either way—those determine which standard actually governs. Worthiness is built in those moments. Esteem is irrelevant to them.

How to Apply This Today

Think of three decisions from the past week made when no one significant would notice the outcome either way. Were those decisions made by the same standard as the ones made in visible situations?

The gap—if one exists—is the gap between what's being performed and what's actually been integrated. No judgment on either side of it. Just clarity about where the standard actually sits, and where work remains.

"To the man who controls himself, the world is too small an obstacle."

Discourses 3.22.18

What Epictetus Meant

Common experience runs the other way: the world presents obstacles, and the person is either equal to them or not. This inverts it. What determines whether obstacles prevail isn't their size but where the locus of control sits. Someone who has established authority over their own judgment encounters the world's obstacles from a different position than someone who hasn't. The obstacle is the same. The position is different.

"Controls himself" isn't suppression or stoic performance. It's the practical result of everything that precedes: judgment that holds, attention that's been trained, standards that don't renegotiate when convenience presses. Those who've actually built this don't encounter obstacles as tests of endurance. They encounter them as conditions requiring appropriate response. The world hasn't shrunk. The relationship to it has changed.

Why This Still Matters

Difficulty feels disproportionate when it meets a self that's been partially built. The standards are real in principle but haven't been integrated in practice. Pressure then finds the gaps—places where training stopped, where standards are held theoretically but not yet habitually. Integration closes those gaps, not because difficulty stops arriving, but because the response to it has been settled in advance.

How to Apply This Today

Identify the kind of difficulty that most reliably disrupts your judgment—the category where composure fails, where standards bend, where the response doesn't match what you'd endorse in a calmer moment.

That's the unintegrated portion. Not a character failure—an area where practice hasn't reached yet. Treat it as such: the next instance isn't a test to pass or fail, it's a training session for the specific gap. What would integrated response look like there?

Not suppression—the same steadiness that appears in easier situations, extended to this one.

"No man is free who is not master of himself."

Discourses 4.1.52

What Epictetus Meant

Self-mastery is the precondition of freedom, not its consequence. Freedom that depends on external conditions—favorable circumstances, others' cooperation, absence of opposition—isn't freedom. It's favorable weather. Self-mastery is the only form of freedom that survives variation in conditions, because it isn't located where conditions can reach it.

"Master of himself" means what the preceding chapters describe: judgment that holds, assent withheld until examination is complete, desire placed where it can be satisfied through choice, attention trained to return. Each of those capacities is a dimension of the mastery being named here. Together, they constitute a self that can be governed—not rigidly, but reliably.

Why This Still Matters

Freedom is usually sought in conditions: fewer constraints, more options, better circumstances. The search is indefinite because conditions never stabilize completely. Self-mastery offers a different kind of freedom—available regardless of conditions, because it doesn't depend on them.

Those who have it don't require circumstances to be right before engaging fully. They bring the same quality of judgment to difficult conditions as to easy ones, because the standard isn't calibrated to conditions.

How to Apply This Today

Name one external condition you're currently treating as a prerequisite for operating at your best. More time. Better support. Reduced pressure. A different environment.

Now ask: what would change in your conduct if that condition were permanently unavailable? If the answer is "I'd operate at a lower level," the condition is governing judgment. That's the dependency. Self-mastery here means developing the capacity to operate at the same level regardless—not by forcing it, but by training judgment to function without the prerequisite.

"The noblest thing is to contend with yourself."

Discourses 3.13.13

What Epictetus Meant

The competition that matters is internal. Not comparison with others—competition with your own previous standard. Each day provides the same contest: does judgment hold as well as it did yesterday, better, or worse? External comparison misleads because others' standards are unknown and irrelevant to the measure that actually governs you. Internal competition is precise: you know what your standard is, you know what last week produced, you know where consistency held and where it didn't.

"Contend with yourself" isn't self-criticism. It's engagement with the actual contest. The work of integrated discipline isn't impressive to outside observers and isn't meant to be. It's the private work of holding the standard higher than it was, in small increments, consistently. That's where character is built and where it's maintained.

Why This Still Matters

The pull toward comparison with others is constant. Status, progress, recognition—all measured relative to what others are doing. That comparison produces either complacency or envy, neither of which improves judgment. The internal contest produces something different: clarity about the specific gap between current standard and possible standard, and the motion to close it through practice rather than through performance.

How to Apply This Today

At the end of each day this week, ask one question: "Did my judgment hold better or worse today than yesterday in the areas that matter?" Not a score—a direction.

If worse, identify specifically where. Not to criticize—to locate what needs practice tomorrow. If better, identify why. What held that previously didn't? That's the capacity being built. The contest is only with the previous version of the standard. Everything else is noise.

"In theory there is nothing to prevent our following the precepts of philosophy; in practice, however, it is difficult."

Discourses 2.9.13

What Epictetus Meant

The distance between understanding and application is named directly. Not as failure or discouragement—as fact. The precepts are clear. What stands between clarity and conduct is practice: the repeated return to standard, the corrected attention, the withheld assent, the maintained posture under conditions that press against it.

This statement belongs in a closing chapter because it prevents the mistake of treating what precedes as complete once understood. Understanding doesn't close the gap. Only application does—repeated, imperfect, corrected. The person who has understood the ideas and the person who has practiced them enough to carry them under pressure are not in the same position. That distance closes only one way.

Why This Still Matters

The final failure of most discipline projects is substitution: understanding replaces application. The material has been read, the principle grasped, the logic followed. The work feels done. But the gap between knowing and holding hasn't moved. Difficulty arrives, and the understanding is present—the capacity isn't. The principle didn't transfer. The practice hadn't happened.

No summary here pretends the work is done. It's ongoing, and continuation requires what's always required—practice in the small things, correction of the small lapses, attention returned each time it drifts.

How to Apply This Today

Take one principle from this book that you understand clearly—where the logic is solid and the reasoning is followed. Now ask: in the last week, did your conduct actually reflect it, or did you understand it while behaving otherwise?

The gap between those two, wherever it appears, is where the work is. Not the understanding—that's complete. The practice. Name one specific situation in the coming week where you'll apply that principle deliberately. Not as performance—as the continuation of training that was always the point.

"When you are going about any action, remind yourself of what the action is. If you are going to bathe, put to yourself the incidents usual in the bath: some persons ill, others biting, others stealing. And thus you will more safely go about the action."

Enchiridion 4

What Epictetus Meant

Preparation is the final discipline. Not pessimism—accurate expectation. Before any significant engagement, judgment is positioned correctly by running through what is likely to be encountered. Not so that difficulty can be avoided, but so that when it arrives, it doesn't arrive as surprise. Surprise is what gives difficulty its leverage. An expected difficulty is a known condition requiring response. An unexpected one presses judgment before it's oriented.

The bath is deliberately mundane. Preparation isn't only for battle or major loss—it applies to an ordinary errand, because the discipline practiced in ordinary situations is what's available in significant ones. The habit is built where it seems least necessary, which is exactly where it has to be built.

Why This Still Matters

Disruption costs most when it's treated as exceptional. The rude person, the delayed plan, the obstacle mid-execution—ordinary features of action that unprepared judgment encounters as affronts. The same features, anticipated, become conditions to work with rather than problems to protest.

This is where the book ends because it's where each day begins: before the action, not after it. What is likely to happen? What response would judgment, operating correctly, produce? The preparation doesn't guarantee the response. It makes it available.

How to Apply This Today

Before any significant engagement tomorrow—a difficult conversation, a demanding task, a situation where composure is likely to be tested—spend two minutes running through what's ordinarily difficult about this kind of thing.

The colleague who interrupts. The plan that shifts mid-execution. The response that doesn't arrive as expected. Name them, not to dread them—to remove their power to surprise. Then proceed. Judgment that expected difficulty encounters it as a known condition. Judgment that didn't encounters the same thing as a disruption. The situation is identical. The preparation determines which.

Appendix — Primary Sources

The quotes in this book are drawn from two texts: the *Enchiridion* and the *Discourses*. Both are available in full, in multiple English translations, at no cost.

Reading them directly is the next step. Not to find more material, but to encounter Epictetus without the mediation of commentary—including this book's. The rules he sets down are meant to be handled, not discussed. The originals make that clear in a way no secondary source can replicate.

Scan the QR codes below to access the public-domain sources hosted on Archive.org.

Enchiridion

Discourses

Thanks

Thank you for spending time with this book. Reading with attention is a deliberate act, and I respect the discipline it requires. I hope these pages helped sharpen judgment rather than add commentary, and offered something usable rather than merely agreeable.

My thanks go to the collaborators at Karma Studio, whose careful work and steady reliability supported this project from beginning to end. I am also grateful to Giulio Vitali, author of *Vox Populi*, for his clear guidance and measured counsel throughout the development of this book.

I thank my family as well, for their patience during the time and focus this work demanded. Their support made sustained attention possible.

If you found this book useful and are inclined to do so, an honest review on Amazon would be appreciated. Reviews support independent authors and help other readers decide whether this book aligns with what they are seeking.

Thank you for reading.

— *Richard Lawson*